educational
media and
the teacher

ISSUES AND INNOVATIONS IN EDUCATION

Consulting Editor
JOSEPH C. BENTLEY
The University of Utah

Expanding the Self: Personal Growth for Teachers—
*Angelo V. Boy and Gerald J. Pine, University of
New Hampshire*

Changing Student Behavior: A New Approach to
Discipline—*Duane Brown, West Virginia University*

Classroom Evaluation for Teachers—*Henry Dizney,
University of Oregon*

Compensatory Programming: The Acid Test of
American Education—*Joe L. Frost, The University
of Texas at Austin, and G. Thomas Rowland, The
Institute for Epistemic Studies*

Educational Media and the Teacher—*John B. Haney,
University of Illinois at Chicago Circle, and
Eldon J. Ullmer, The Florida State University*

Motivation—*Ivan L. Russell, University of Missouri—
St. Louis*

Group Processes in the Classroom—*Richard A.
Schmuck, University of Oregon, and Patricia A.
Schmuck*

Encouraging Creativity in the Classroom—*E. Paul
Torrance, University of Georgia*

educational media
and the teacher

John B. Haney
*Queens College of the City University
of New York*

Eldon J. Ullmer
*University of Wisconsin—
Oshkosh*

WM. C. BROWN COMPANY PUBLISHERS
Dubuque, Iowa

Fifth Printing, 1972

Printed in the United States of America

11/25/75 *Becker b Zgler* 2.2r

Contents

Preface

When encountering any new book treating recent developments in education, the teacher is justified in asking, "How does this apply to me? How can it help me do my job?"

This introductory book on educational media seeks to bridge the gap between short audiovisual equipment guides and materials brochures on the one hand, and weighty voluminous texts on the other. Our concern is with what the pre-service and in-service teacher wants and needs to know about the effective use of media. Our aim has been to present it in a form that is clear, concise, accurate, and—above all—useful.

In keeping with this approach, the emphasis on theory and process, as evidenced in the first three chapters, is deliberate. There is nothing more practical in the long run than sound theory and valid action principles. Chapter 1 explores how media and technology affect the educative process involving both pupils and teachers. Chapters 2 and 3 review human learning and the communication characteristics and capabilities of educational media relating to the task of designing instruction. Our focus is always on the systematic employment of media and materials, centering on the teacher as a strategist and manager of the learning environment.

The book stresses a variety of approaches, not laying down rules as much as indicating possibilities for imaginative and purposeful utilization of the newer educational media in elementary and secondary schools. Also, the book presents concrete information as to what the teacher can do independently in working with equipment, selecting or producing materials, and obtaining the assistance of professional media specialists in his school building or district media center.

In a field where there are as many continuing developments as there are in educational media, a book which dwells on the specifics of particular types of equipment or methods of production has a "half-life" of only a couple of years. Every year, at the conventions of the national associations in the media field, new technological wonders are brought forth that render the current devices obsolescent or, at the least, outdated. By means of theory and principles, all new developments can be placed in context, and the reader is prepared to expect and to cope with change.

J. B. H.
E. J. U.

ACKNOWLEDGMENTS

Many persons contributed to the preparation of this book during the successive approximations that constituted the process of development. The manuscript was read and commented upon by teachers with experience at various levels; by specialists in media design, production, and administration; and by students in teacher preparation programs. All of these people provided valuable feedback as to the contributions of the volume to the actual tasks faced by teachers in using media in real classroom situations. In this regard, particular thanks is owed Mr. Robert Schneider, Dr. Mary Alice Mayer, and Sister Mary Matthew Donovan. The authors also wish to acknowledge with appreciation the editorial assistance of Diane Haney and B. Joyce Shafer.

The photographs illustrating the topics covered in this book were obtained from a variety of sources. These are indicated with each illustration. UICC refers to the University of Illinois at Chicago Circle, Edward J. Retel, Jr., photographer. Other photographs were supplied and used through the courtesy of manufacturers of illustrated equipment and materials, or of educators and institutions that hold releases, clearances, and in certain cases, copyrights thereon. None can be further reproduced without written permission of the indicated source.

DEDICATION

To Earl M. Haney, who has been teacher of mathematics to two generations of pupils at Washington High School, Milwaukee, Wisconsin,

1

Teachers and Pupils
in a Mediated Environment

Modern communications media act as social, cultural, and educational forces in and out of school, affecting the roles and stature of both teachers and pupils. The very pervasiveness of media in contemporary society tends to obscure the nature of their power, but an understanding of this power can be developed by looking at some of the effects of media on our everyday relationships and experiences.

The Child and Media

Teachers today are constantly amazed at what children already know about what they are going to be taught. Upon holding up pictures of prehistoric scenes, a third grade teacher may find her pupils identifying dinosaurs such as the brontosaurus, the tyrannosaurus rex, and the triceratops, and wondering where the pterodactyls went. When introducing number concepts, the first grade teacher may find children counting 10-9-8-7-6-5-4-3-2-1-0, which, to the teacher, is counting backwards. To the child, this is counting *toward* something; "regular" counting (1-2-3-4-5-6-7-8-9-10) is counting *away* from something, and both are as natural as breathing out and breathing in. When the general science teacher begins to explain the eclipses of the sun and moon, the pupils usually can fill in any missing details of the relative positions and relevant forces, for they have themselves, in mediated fashion, been to the moon and back.

Virtually the whole world of experience is available to the child in mediated form. By the time a youth graduates from high school today, he has viewed approximately 15,000 hours of television and has attended 500 feature motion pictures. During the same years, he has spent just 11,000 hours in the classroom. The time spent viewing television and films is an important factor in itself, irrespective of the content. It is time that is not spent in some other way.

1

"Gee whizz, Pop, we've seen this before!"

Drawing by Lorenz; © 1969
The New Yorker Magazine, Inc.

More than quantitative figures, the qualitative nature of the child's experience with the media is important. The distinguished American architect and designer, Buckminster Fuller, calls television "the third parent." When a child is plopped in front of the television set and left on his own for hours, he witnesses family squabbles, physical violence, the commission of crimes, and anything else the fiction writers can think of. For that matter, the content of news broadcasts—war, crime, rioting, and the like—is often powerful fare for young minds. As McLuhan says, "Only bad news is news; good news is advertising or public relations." So today's maturing child has a tremendous knowledge of world events, personalities, and problems, and probably a better understanding of human nature. He tends to think of the "big problems": how to handle the recurring armed conflicts; what to do in space exploration; how to change the government of the country. The "little problems" of home and office he leaves to his parents.

This exposure to the world at large tends to broaden the sources of influence on children. In the old days, the family, the church, and the school constituted the big three in terms of influencing a child's development. This is not true to the same degree anymore. In addition to these traditional sources, he now hears from many experts and authorities. The mass media no doubt affect his concept of authority and his capacity for trust. In the age of "the fix," "payola," and "managed news," he learns to be skeptical of almost all communication. Not long ago, if one could say, "It's true; I saw it in black and white," the argument was over; this was considered indisputable. Today such a statement would be considered laughable. The modern youth is all too well aware of what it means to have "a vested interest" or "an axe to grind."

The effect of mass communications media can be viewed as a distinct social process. Janowitz and Street identify three functions of media within this context: providing information, socializing, and mobilizing.

> By the information function, we mean the transmission and dissemination of information and essential knowledge, and the posing of alternatives for economic, social, and political action. By the socialization function, we mean the transmission of a cultural system, and the inculcation of values and norms which make possible a person's participation in a variety of social groupings—from the family to the nation-state. By the mobilization function, we refer to the processes of persuasion and the development of loyalties and attachments which are essential for collective problem solving.[1]

PROVIDING INFORMATION. Educators have performed considerable amounts of research on the value of the new media in achieving the first function, that of transmitting information. Tests of verbal knowledge indicate that the new media indeed can provide for learning in almost any subject matter, with almost any group of learners, in almost any place, and at virtually any time of the day or night. This is hardly news.

Much less is known, however, about the contributions of media to the other two functions. But, of course, this is not an easy area in which to do research. It is very difficult, if not impossible, to gauge the effect of media among several factors—heredity, environment, religion, ethnic background, family structure—in an individual's social and cultural makeup. But some observations can be made with a reasonable degree of certainty.

SOCIALIZING. The media instantly communicate new fads, clothing styles, music, art, and even life styles. One year, everyone is saying: "Would you believe. . . .?"; the next year, it's "Sock it to me." Someone recently said that this is the first generation in which the young are the same all over the world. What happens in one neighborhood, or country, for that matter, becomes community property in the global village. As the young become increasingly unified through media while the old retain their traditional differences, the generation gap widens.

---

[1]Morris Janowitz and David Street, "The Social Organization of Education," in *The New Media and Education,* eds. Peter H. Rossi and Bruce J. Biddle (Garden City, N. Y.: Doubleday & Co., 1967), p. 230. (Originally published by Aldine Publishing Co., Chicago, 1966.)

The "all-at-onceness" of modern communications media seems to instill in people a feeling of "It's got to be now." Investors want to double their money overnight. "Fly now, pay later" the travel ads say. New art forms do not progress from a beginning, through a middle, to an end. They just happen. Small wonder that children are discouraged at the prospect of sitting at a desk for twelve years of rigidly sequenced education. Their preschool learning took place in a highly mediated, high information density, unstructured environment. The school should add structure and direction to the learning process, but not by decreasing the level of information available to children or by relying on print and speech as the only media forms in regular use.

The media can greatly affect the way in which children, and adults, see their fellow human beings. Consider the stereotyped portrayals of black Americans in films and television, and the change in effect when the black militants begin appearing on the screen. What generalizations about the problems of minority groups might children make when they see that, in one country, white Catholics are voicing complaints and demands similar to those that Negroes are making in their own country?

Thus the socializing effects of media on the young are largely those of increasing awareness of world affairs, increasing identification with world problems, and increasing desire for involvement in change. The interaction of this mentality with the more detached personality of previous print-fed generations is one of the most significant and volatile phenomenons of the present era.

MOBILIZING. The mobilizing powers of media would seem to be considerable. An entire nation stops what it is doing as millions watch on television the funeral of a political leader. Large numbers of people are impelled to travel long distances to participate in demonstrations of one type or another. Media reporting of certain events such as riots and warfare may serve as training films for impressionable youth who are motivated to try similar tactics in their own neighborhood. And, of course, the power of advertising media to mobilize consumers is well known.

Media Effects on the Role of the Teacher

The recent emphasis on science, technology, and other academic study has resulted in a tremendous acceleration in both the rate and the amount of knowledge available in print and in other media forms. It is probably safe to say that in many fields, half of the existing knowledge has been accumulated in the past ten to fifteen years.

This fact has a very important implication for school curriculum design, which can no longer be approached as a process of sequencing

The newer educational media in full application in the schools markedly affect the traditional roles of teachers and pupils.

everything worth knowing. Thus educators must be very selective in choosing the content to be learned in schools. The goal is no longer to have pupils store away vast amounts of information. Higher level competencies must be developed. The ability to analyze and evaluate existing knowledge; to recognize patterns in masses of raw data; to apply knowledge to new situations; to use it in making strategies and solving problems—these are the skills that must be cultivated.

In this age of rapid expansion of knowledge, a scholar can be defined as one who is growing ignorant at a less rapid rate than others. The teacher can no longer act as the authority on all facts. He must become a guide and counselor to the pupil, a manager of the learning situation, a commentator on world affairs, and a model of intellectual activity. His work is truly professional and more than a little difficult. From the vast array of content, he must select objectives that are worthwhile but feasible; he must decide how learner competence will be judged; he must structure sequences of learning events that will be effective in bringing about these competencies. To do this, he must learn how to select from the vast array of educational media and methods available. Now the teacher is truly a professional. Anyone can show and tell. To take responsibility for learning is another matter.

The average child has quite an information center in his own home. One or two television sets is typical. He has a radio in the living room, the bedroom, the car, and possibly around his neck. And there is a steady flow of newspapers and magazines. The average youth also attends the movies with regularity. No wonder he is said to be "plugged in" or "turned on." Anything that goes on in the world he makes his business. He is truly a member of the global village.

The school should attempt to emulate this "turned on" environment to a certain degree. This does not mean that it should adopt a "show biz" format. Learning is quite different from entertainment. But today's pupil will no longer sit still for routine drill. The teacher should utilize every means at his disposal to make education interesting, vivid, and involving. If he is not "turned on," he may be "tuned out."

If the child has all these options for gaining information outside the school, surely he should have them in school, as well. There are several alternative ways that media can be employed to provide pupils with learning opportunities. Media can be piped into a classroom as with broadcast television, closed circuit television, radio, and public address systems. Media presentations can be offered to an entire class under the control of the teacher, as is customarily done with films. Media presentations can be offered in a learning center on a repeating basis for independent reception by individuals or small groups. And media can be used independently and individually as in a study carrel or a language laboratory.

Thus a teacher is asking too much of himself to try personally to provide all the stimuli required for learning. Let the media do it. The teacher's job is to organize the circumstances that provide the best opportunity for learning and to ensure that learning takes place. He can ease his own burden if he uses media to its best advantage and builds replicable instructional episodes around media forms that can be repeated for successive classes. In plain talk, once he has the "system working," he can spend less time talking and more time on planning and evaluation. He can cease being a drill sergeant and become instead an education executive.

Media Effects on Children in School

The variety of media now available to the teacher provides him with powerful and flexible communications tools. These media also can significantly affect the quality of learning experiences for pupils. Media can provide rich visual experiences not possible without them. They extend the normal limits of communication through the use of films about foreign lands, videotapes of great personalities, live telecasts of important events, and many other types of uses. Some media enable teachers to communicate to large numbers of children simultaneously and thus extend their influence. Media offer communications advantages in terms of physical control of stimuli. Magnification enables an entire audience to have a front row seat at a demonstration. Slow motion and stop-action enable closer analysis to be made of dynamic phenomena. Time lapse photography provides for rapid viewing of processes that actually occur over long periods of time. Media can supply multisensory stimuli and multi-image stimuli, thus enabling the matching of audio and visual and the comparing or contrasting of visual phenomena. Media serve as storage banks of information, easily retrievable for display in the classroom. Media also provide a vehicle for pupils to participate in creative expression by making their own materials, either for teaching purposes or for pupil projects.

As the teacher can change his own role through the systematic use of media, so will the pupils' conception of that role likely be different in a highly mediated school environment. Hopefully, the child will view the teacher as a resource person, a guide and counselor, rather than just as a dispenser of information.

Media can affect the relationship of classmates to each other as they participate in the learning process. In the traditional classroom, pupils sit still and follow in unison the lecture or whatever presentation is made. The progress of the class must be held down to that of the slowest members of the group. This can be a source of irritation to the brighter pupils and a cause of embarrassment to the slower learners. If the teacher tries to maintain a happy medium, he might lose people at both ends.

Media can be used to allow pupils more independent study and thus break away from lock-step learning. If there are extensive media resources available in a school, greater flexibility can be built into the teaching program in terms of providing for independent learning; of allowing individual pupils to work on special projects; and of producing materials for media as a form of work. As learning becomes increasingly individualized through media utilization, pupils need not feel held back by their classmates, nor will they feel the competition for grades that is now so prevalent. Pupils should be evaluated in relation to the quality of their work, not in relation to each other. Thus a more relaxed relationship among class members could be fostered by the growth of individualized, mediated instruction.

As learners gain increasing proficiency in teaching themselves with media, so will they be able to develop individual interests and talents and thus amplify their differences from other pupils. This occurrence contrasts significantly from the common practice of leading every pupil through the same content in the same time period. A key feature of using media is flexibility. The availability of numerous form of new media, such as film loops, filmstrips, synchronized slide tapes, dial access gear, and new methods of display and control, enable the teacher to emerge from the traditional lecture-discussion format and give much more varied and individualized instruction.

This general discussion of the broad functions of media provides the context for showing how media can be beneficial to the educational process.

2

The Bases for the Educational Use of Media

Theories Relevant to Media Application

There are several theories of education, or learning theories, that have affected educational practice through the years. These same theories also have an effect on media utilization in education because they influence the way that writers and producers create materials and the way that teachers evaluate and utilize materials. Accordingly, it will be helpful to examine several of the most popular of these theories.

STIMULUS-RESPONSE THEORY. This is a behavioristic and somewhat mechanistic approach in which habit plays a central role. In brief, this theory says that learning is a change in behavior and that the teacher has two tasks: first to decide what behavior is to be expected of pupils, or what behavior will be accepted as evidence that desired learning has taken place; and then to teach the behavior directly.

According to the stimulus-response theory, there are four elements to learning: *Drive*—the learner must feel a need for something or want something; *Stimulus or Cue*—the learner must notice something or be presented with a message; *Response*—the learner reacts to the stimulus; *Reward*—the learner is given something for making the correct response.

In this theory, education consists of bringing prescribed responses under the control of appropriate stimuli by arranging contingencies that reinforce desired behavior. Complex behavior patterns are built up step by step from simpler forms of behavior. The application of this theory is best exemplified by some types of programmed instruction in which pupils must make frequent responses, and in which correct responses are immediately reinforced. The knowledge of having made a correct response is presumed to be satisfying and thus serves as reward to motivate the learner.

9

PERCEPTION THEORY. This viewpoint holds that perception and cognitive processes are the foundation of learning. The senses are regarded as perceptual mechanisms that enable use to know our external environment. The mind serves as a cognitive mechanism which somehow processes varied perceptions into specific concepts and understandings. These understandings are essential to thinking, and thinking, in turn, aids in the development of attitudes, appreciations, and the like.

In this philosophy of education, providing rich sensory experiences becomes a vital element. Media are viewed as excellent vehicles for providing experiences that are "concrete" and "realistic." Not too much emphasis is given to requiring specific responses to specific stimuli, because it is felt that individual learners will perceive things differently and respond differently according to their culture, background, and previous experiences. It is presumed that the more real and concrete the learning experience, the better will pupils be able to develop understandings and therefore the better will they be able to think and to solve their problems. Thus the use of lifelike media materials is encouraged as a basis for more abstract learning, and a much less rigorous attitude is adopted toward measuring behavior change resulting from such usage than in the stimulus-response framework.

INFORMATION THEORY. Information theory provides a more mathematical view of human communication and has as its central concepts *channel capacity, redundancy,* and *noise. Channel capacity* is the highest rate at which a communications channel can transmit information. *Redundancy* is a characteristic of message construction referring to the repetition of stimulus arrays and resultant increase in the number of learning trials or opportunities. *Noise* is the name applied to all competing stimuli which interfere with the transmission of a message. Noise, obviously, does not originate with the sender and includes sound, physical discomfort, viewer tension or anxiety, or anything else that might detract from the message.

Information theory has not had much effect on educational practice or on the production of media materials. If, however, as some psychologists maintain, the human being performs as a single channel receiver, the concepts of channel capacity and redundancy do have relevance to the ability of viewers to learn from media. It certainly appears that a great proportion of materials produced move at too fast a rate for comprehension and that they might have been better designed if these concepts, *channel capacity, redundancy,* and *noise,* had been considered.

PERSONALITY THEORY. Another group of psychologists, called personality theorists, denies that biological drives have a unique function in motivating human behavior. They say, rather, that several factors are necessary to account for such behavior and that these factors include *motivation, expectancy,* and *incentive. Motivation* is defined as a readiness to act; the learner is in a state of anticipating some goal. *Expectancy* is defined as the individual's belief in his own ability to achieve success in attaining the goal. The variable *incentive* represents the relative attractiveness of the goal. This theory clearly introduces considerations of learner personality and values into the learning equation. To cope with these factors requires more than the efficient structuring of stimulus-response events or the application of mathematical guides to message construction.

Learning Theories and Media Utilization

Teachers are probably not so much interested in theories as they are in getting their job done. And probably none of the above theories provides a complete basis for educational practice although each seems to have something to contribute. An individual who is strongly committed to one of these theories will undoubtedly be affected by that theory in the way he approaches educational tasks, either as a teacher using media or as a writer or producer creating materials. In general, these various theories will tend to cause producers and teachers to adopt one of two orientations toward the creation and use of media materials. One can be termed a stimulus or perceptual view and the other the behavioral view.

In creating or selecting media materials from the stimulus viewpoint, primary consideration is given to the technical or message characteristics of the materials. Interesting content, careful writing, fine photography, and good picture composition are considered as being highly important. Excellence in materials is judged, by producers and teachers, in terms of their being clear, exciting, moving, or stimulating to *them* and their colleagues. The behavioral orientation places less concern on these types of criteria; of prime importance is the question: "Does the material produce the kind of behavior *in children* that it was designed to produce?"

Materials producers holding to a stimulus or perceptual view tend to create programs rich in sensory stimuli. They often utilize multimedia presentations in which several images can be directed to the pupil simultaneously. They tend to think of using visuals to illustrate concepts rather than to enable learners to acquire specific behavioral responses. Learner participation would normally be expected to take place in some followup activity *after* the presentation.

Producers favoring a stimulus-response view tend to create materials that incorporate direct practice of desired learner behavior, in the presence of specific stimuli, *during* the program. They tend to include stimuli for which desired responses can be measured and validated and to exclude stimuli for which such measurement is difficult or unpredictable. When scripting or programming, the behaviorist questions each item of content in terms of its contribution to the final learner behavior. Special effects, or other embellishments that many television and film producers consider useful in making a presentation more interesting and enjoyable, would be considered superfluous by most behaviorists if these embellishments had no effect on behavior change.

Which of these two theoretical orientations is favored by a teacher will obviously affect the way he approaches his work and the way he employs media in the classroom. The behaviorist would likely say that the principal reason for using visual media is to enable the learner to make visual discriminations, that is, make identifications of specific visual phenomena in the presence of other visual stimuli that are potentially confusing. Naming different types of plants, identifying different organs of the body, identifying cells that are healthy or diseased, discriminating between the two types of camels, dromedary and Bactrian—all these identifications require the learner to make visual discriminations.

The stimulus oriented teacher will likely take a less structured view. He will, of course, test some learning as outcomes of media presentations, but mainly he will use visual media to show what something looks like or to provide more concrete experience. He sees media presentations as contributing to a variety of abilities, attitudes, and values and would likely consider it an impractical task to try and make accurate measurements of all these effects. His technique is less certain than the behaviorist's, but it is more opportunistic.

Thus one's theoretical orientation and philosophy of education can greatly affect his approach to producing, evaluating, and using media materials. Each teacher must decide for himself just what orientation or blend of theory he will bring to his teaching and to media utilization.

Roles of Educational Media

Media can play several roles in the educational process, and it is important to identify them because they make a difference in the way one plans to use media and in the type of outcome expected. Also, it seems that some writers tend to confuse the concepts of media roles and media capabilities. Such phrases as the "ability to overcome limitations of time and space" or "to extend the horizons of the learner" refer to capabilities of media. The term "role" as used here refers to the type of effect or function involved in media utilization and includes consideration of the types of relationship of media, content, and learner. Therefore, the most common roles served by media are instruction, dramatization, documentation, performance analysis, simulation, and as vehicles for creative expression for learners.

An instructional use is one in which media is used with the intent of achieving specific learning that can be identified and on which learners will be tested. And so an instructional instrument is one which has been designed and validated to bring about specific changes in learner competency. The most common examples of such instruments are the programs designed according to the principles of programmed instruction. Such design and validation techniques need not be limited to the print medium, however.

A dramatization is, of course, most commonly a film or videotape of a literary production or a historical reenactment. It enables pupils to see the great literature of the world acted out or to be present at important historical events of the past. But media can also be used to dramatize phenomena such as the territorial behavior of animals, or to portray the struggles of a scientist trying to find a cure for a dreaded disease, or the suffering and despair of a poverty-stricken family.

A documentary is an accurate recording of some event or phenomenon as it occurs or exists, and primary concern is given to the accuracy and realism of the recording. Unlike an instructional program, the potential uses for a documentary should be secondary in the minds of the producers. For example, if one is shooting a documentary on the life of a soldier in combat, the prime concern should be on realistically recording what the soldier's life is like without considering whether different people might use the film as a propaganda vehicle, a training vehicle, a political campaign ad, or as encouragement to buy saving bonds.

Performance analysis refers to the practice of using media to record the performance of a learner in such areas as teacher training, speech, drama, dance, sports, medicine, and so forth. Small videotape recorders are especially valuable for this application because they are portable, they do not require a large crew, and it is easy to play back a performance for analysis of techniques that need to be improved or corrected.

Media can be used in the classroom to simulate some external situation, as with driver training devices, mock-ups, and so forth. Also, media can be used to simulate planning or decision making situations.

Another important role for media in the classroom is to serve as a source of pupil involvement, motivation, and expression when learners produce materials for use in the classroom. Pupils can produce materials to be used in their own education or as an assignment or project. They can also explore and document activities in their own communities. With the low cost of some present-day 35mm cameras and 8mm motion picture equipment, this type of media use is becoming increasingly widespread. If pupils are involved in their own education through this type of activity, their interest and motivation is likely to be enhanced considerably and their ability to communicate increased as well.

Media Characteristics and Capabilities

The term medium (or media) has come to apply to a great many things which have communicative capabilities. In education, when we think of media we usually think of films, television, slides, filmstrips, audiotapes, records, and various combinations of these things. Many other types of media have application to education, including, graphic materials, display materials, the chalkboard, maps and globes, models, mock-ups, realia, exhibits, and games.

CHARACTERISTICS OF MEDIA. The many different communications instruments that are termed media obviously possess widely different characteristics. Consequently, there are many different ways of looking at or categorizing these media. Media take different physical forms: they can be made of paper, transparent plastic, film, or magnetic tape. Different media obviously involve different senses by presenting stimuli that are auditory, visual, or both. Media have been referred to as being either static or dynamic, that is, either they can or they can not depict motion. Some media, such as radio and television, have been labeled "mass media," whereas others are thought of as individual or small group media. And media can be labeled as being permanent or transient in terms of the duration of their display. A film is transient in terms of display but permanent in terms of storage.

The attempt to bring some order to the analysis of these varied media characteristics may be served by considering them in three categories: capability for verbal communication; capability for pictorial display (the term *visual* is avoided because print is both verbal and visual); and characteristics related to instructional effectiveness and functional applications.

The verbal communications characteristics of the various kinds of print media are quite obvious. It should be pointed out, however, that verbal information—captions, titles, labels—can be effectively used as typographical elements in films, slides, transparencies, and other primarily visual media.

The most important capabilities related to pictorial display are depicting black and white, color, movement, enlargement, reduction, and whether the visual sequence is fixed or flexible. Obviously, all media display in black and white and all photographic media—book illustrations, slides, filmstrips, and films—can be made in color. Color television is now available at a price that educational institutions can afford. All photographic media also provide the capability either to enlarge or to reduce an image. Television can also display enlargements by use of a close-up lens or a microscope. Television and films provide the realistic appearance of motion, whereas the other media do not. Artistic techniques can be used in still pictures to illustrate that motion is taking place, however. Television, motion pictures, and filmstrips have a fixed visual sequence and, except for silent filmstrips, a fixed rate of presentation. Slides and illustrated books, as well as individual still photographs provide for flexible sequencing, flexible pacing, and, therefore, unlimited referability. For these reasons, these pictorial media have a big advantage in terms of accommodating the varied needs of pupils for different amounts of exposure or greater numbers of learning trials.

In addition to the mere capability for display, there are characteristics of media related to the conditions for controlling displays and for involving learner participation in the learning event. These are very important characteristics from the standpoint of learning effectiveness. Most of the traditional audiovisual media materials are geared to a fixed-pace, one-time showing type of presentation. A film, for example, is usually run from beginning to end with no variation in the duration of display and usually no opportunity for learner participation. It gives all viewers identical treatment. The duration of a film is usually determined by the length of time it takes to cover a topic, not by the length of time it takes pupils to learn a given amount of knowledge. Thus, when using a film, a teacher must be careful to coordinate suitable complementary events or activities to ensure that the desired learning takes place. And so such materials as films, television videotapes, audiotapes, and sound filmstrips can be said to be *internally paced* in that the teacher, or viewers, cannot control the display other than by starting and stopping a machine. On the other hand, ordinary textbooks allow the user complete freedom to repeat and review material at will and also to study verbal or pictorial stimuli for as long as necessary. In addition, programmed texts make systematic provision for learner response, and so combine the desirable characteristics of being externally, or learner, paced and of requiring overt learner participation.

Another important instructional characteristic of media is the facility for cuing learner responses, both verbal and non-verbal. Verbal responses, if they are relatively brief, can be incorporated into virtually any type of media, although some are more advantageous than others. Television does not have a high definition picture, and with the relatively small screen size, it is not well suited to displaying large amounts of print. This may be a handicap in some presentations. Slides, in the 35mm format, are also handicapped in this sense because the image size is so small. Overhead transparencies and 3¼x4 inch slides are excellent for displaying substantial amounts of print at one time. Therefore, if a teacher wishes to use multiple-choice questions, for example, these media would be very useful. Programmed texts are obviously excellent media forms for cuing verbal responses. They can also readily be used to facilitate nonverbal participation, as learning some procedure or performing some manipulative skill. The audiotutorial approach, which is really more than one medium, is an excellent technique for involving learners in a variety of participating experiences all the way from taking notes or filling in blanks to performing some experiment.

Any conception of an ideal teaching system would include the condition that the system be adaptive to learner responses. The teacher does this by asking questions and by reading "question marks" on the faces of pupils listening to his presentation. In the typical classroom, however, the teacher can rarely take the time to be absolutely certain that he is adapting his presentation to meet the learning capacity of all his pupils. Still, experienced teachers do develop this facility. Most media forms used in the classroom have not had any satisfactory way of adapting to learner responses, and the programmed instruction movement represented the first really substantial effort at incorporating this feature into media presentations. The materials which resulted from this effort and which are commonly available to teachers have been largely in the form of programmed texts. However, this feature can be built into almost any media form. Also, experiments with computer assisted instruction have as one of their primary goals the development of individualized teaching systems which are highly adaptable to learner responses. This concern is one of the major thrusts in educational technology today. For today's teacher, using traditional materials in a manner that adapts to the capabilities of individual learners is one of his biggest challenges.

Closely related to the adaptability characteristic is the concern with developing materials that provide immediate feedback to learners with regard to the correctness of their responses. Again, the most common example is the programmed text. Other media can also be used in a manner that provides feedback. One way this is done is with electronic response systems whereby each pupil has a responder unit with approximately four buttons so that he can respond to multiple-choice questions. The teacher without such equipment or programs can still find ways to structure feedback to learners as they work their way through learning experiences. A simple handout may do the job and thus provide for an important characteristic to increase instructional effectiveness.

CAPABILITIES OF MEDIA. Because media may be of such varied form and function, it is difficult to generalize about their capabilities. Writers frequently use such terms as "extending the horizons of pupil experience" or "overcoming time and space" to describe the capabilities of television and motion pictures. While the expressions have become a bit trite, the communications capabilities of these two media are indeed amazing. Such things as satellite transmission of live coverage of events in obscure parts of the earth are now commonplace. Film producers have created virtually any effect one can think of. Consequently, the screen media—films, slides, filmstrips, and television—have tremendous capability in terms of the quality and variety of stimuli they can bring to the classroom, particularly in the visual mode.

Another important capability of media is that they make it possible to have replicable presentations through unlimited repetitions. This, of course, applies to media with permanent storage characteristics. This replicability feature enables a teacher to use media as a self-sufficient communicator during which time he can use his time in some other way, such as interacting with pupils, directing projects, or conducting examinations.

Media are quite valuable because of their capability to regulate and manipulate stimulus control. Besides mere repetition, there are the capabilities provided by time-lapse photography, slow motion, magnification, reverse and repeat features, and even stop action.

Some media have the capability of extending the influence of talented individuals or great teachers to tremendous dimensions. Television broadcasts can reach large numbers of people simultaneously. Films can be duplicated and routed around the world if desired. The same can be said of audiotapes and videotapes. Duplication of media materials makes possible individual instruction in a way that has never been true before.

The Research Base for Audiovisual Communication

Numerous research studies have been made involving the use of media in educational settings. Many of these studies were in the form of comparisons between the results of a course or lesson offered via some media and one offered via traditional instruction. As might be expected, most of these studies show no significant differences in learning. They are valuable, however, in that they provide data to support the general intuitive feeling that people do indeed learn well from media.

However, there have been many studies that dealt with more specific applications of media to particular learning tasks. Most of these have been reported in several summary publications dealing with media in education.

Drawing conclusions from educational studies is a risky business. Often, there are only one or two studies that deal with a specific question or variable. Over the years, there seems to have developed among media enthusiasts a feeling, perhaps based more on faith than on anything else, that because media presentations can combine sight, sound, and motion, they are more concrete and lifelike and consequently effect better learning. For whatever degree of truth there may be in this attitude, it is difficult to measure such generalizations and also difficult to base specific educational practice on them.

If one analyzes the summaries of such studies, however, he will find that they can be grouped into various categories in terms of the central parameter analyzed; and that by examining the outcomes of the studies in each category, some general conclusions can be made. The current body of research literature seems to justify the following conclusions:

1. Adding pictorial material does not necessarily ensure added learning. Most learning in schools is verbal learning, and the evidence does not indicate that pictorial matter aids retention. The pictorial material may well contribute to other types of learning that are not normally measured in highly verbal tests, however. This could be in the form of subtle value orientations or in the power to perceive minute visual and physical differences in objects or phenomena.

2. The value of motion, usually considered as desirable because of its realism, is questionable unless the concept to be learned specifically includes motion as a relevant attribute.

3. With regard to the relative efficiency of auditory and visual channel for transmitting verbal information, no universal conclusion can be drawn because a variety of variables may have different effects in different situations. These include: reading ability—a high reading ability favors the visual channel; I.Q.— a high I.Q. favors the visual channel; degree of organization—the well-organized material favors the audio channel; importance of referability—visual displays have greater referability; meaningfulness of stimulus material—the more meaningful ma-

terials favor the audio channel and conversely, the more ambiguous materials favor the visual channel.

4. The use of color in still visuals may make them more attractive and interesting, but does not necessarily increase learning unless a color discrimination itself is involved or the learner must perceive the dynamic features of an on-going scene.

5. In general, the best learning results from presentations that are simple and direct in approach. Complex arrays, novelty gimmicks, and special effects are not likely to aid learning and may even serve as interference.

6. In film commentaries, studies indicate that verbal simplification procedures tend to increase their teaching effectiveness.

7. There appears to be an optimum rate of speed for verbal narrations, and indications are that this rate should be lowered when audio is accompanied by visualization.

8. The amount of information that can be transmitted to a human receiver appears to be limited and may easily be exceeded by using more than one channel at a time.

9. Audiences can usually profit from repetitions of audiovisual presentations. Those who create media materials, and the teachers who use them, are usually so familiar with the subject themselves that it is often difficult for them to realize that many children cannot learn the lesson in one trial. Many instructional films seem to incorporate insufficient repetition so as to allow most pupils to master specific knowledge and skills dealt with.

10. With regard to learner participation, both overt and covert forms have been found to be effective. Verbalization of response and furnishing knowledge of results are both effective, as is implicit responding or mental practice.

11. The use of pictorial material and color seems to have motivational or interest-producing benefits. However, it appears that interest in a film is not necessarily the same as interest in the subject matter and is not in itself a reliable predictor of resultant learning.

12. In concept learning, the teaching examples should be sufficient in number so that they have only the critical attributes in common.

13. Introductions to audiovisual presentations are most likely to be helpful if they are specific to the learning task by familiarizing the audience with some aspect of the task to be learned or by previewing the task and thus providing an additional learning trial.

14. In situations involving demonstration and practice sessions, it is likely to be more effective if provision is made for practice following each segment of the demonstration rather than having the entire task demonstrated before practice.

3

A Process for Applying
Media Resources to Education

It has been said that there are really only three questions to consider in approaching an instructional task:

What do I want to teach?
How shall I teach it?
How will I know when I have taught it?

To devise an instructional program that effectively meets the requirements suggested by these three questions requires considerable developmental thought and planning. There is a definite process of instructional planning or designing that involves an orderly sequence of activities which are most likely to result in quality instruction. The main phases of this sequence are four.

1. The Specification of Goals and Objectives.
2. The Development of Instructional Strategies.
3. The Implementation of Instruction.
4. The Evaluation of Instruction.

Each of these will be treated in turn.

Educational Objectives: What's It All About?

In the classical developmental sequence, the teacher first sets his objectives; he then selects media, materials, and instructional methods; and finally he carries out and evaluates the instruction. In reality, this does not always happen so neatly. Few teachers have the time to "get away from it all" and think out objectives in great detail. And so, although most people agree that it is desirable to have sound objectives to guide educational activity, not too many teachers have been able to do something really significant about it, at least not in terms of listing detailed objectives for entire courses. Perhaps many of them assume that objectives are inherently clear in the content to be covered, but this is not always true.

Objectives serve several uses in education. They provide a means of communicating to learners and others what is to be achieved during the course. They serve as a basis for selecting media, materials, and instructional methods. And they provide the basis for constructing test items for evaluation purposes. Therefore, clear, specific objectives are an important part of any sound instructional system.

Educational theorists do not all use the same approach to dealing with the problem of objectives; in fact, among them several different approaches are used. One popular classification suggests three basic types: the *cognitive domain,* the *psychomotor domain,* and the *affective domain.* The *cognitive domain* in turn is broken down into several categories: knowledge, comprehension, application, analysis, synthesis, and evaluation. These categories are intended to provide the teacher with a paradigm to construct comprehensive objectives on various levels. They serve to make sure that more than routine objectives are taught and tested. The *psychomotor domain* refers to learning where there is physical activity and skill involved. Objectives in the *affective domain* are those related to acquiring attitudes, values, and the like.

Some scholars, notably psychologists, tend to classify objectives in terms of different types of learning such as learning associations, discriminations, concepts, chains, principles, and problem solving.

In recent years, considerable attention has been given to the practice of stating objectives in "behavioral" terms, based on what the learner will be able to do as a result of instruction. Some controversy has arisen over this issue, with many educators arguing that all learning cannot be explained in terms of behavior. This is probably true. But a teacher is faced with the problem of evaluating learners at a specific time, at the termination of a course of study. Educated guesses and subjective intuition are not a proper basis for this evaluation. Teachers must grade pupils on the basis of performance of some type or other. And so it is to everyone's advantage if the nature of the desired performance is specified with as much detail as is possible. The "performance objective" is the most logical vehicle for doing this.

Although there is considerable disagreement as to what is the most suitable means for handling objectives, several characteristics of the ideal performance objective have been identified. First, the objective should describe the nature of the performance, that is, what the learner must do, in a term that denotes observable behavior. Thus, terms that are not observable, such as *know, understand, grasp,* and *appreciate,* should be avoided, or at least amplified by terms that do denote observable action, such as *write, state, compute, construct, select, identify,* and the like. Secondly, an objective should tell how well the learner must perform and what the standard or level of acceptable performance will be. This can be accomplished with a qualifying statement that indicates a degree of accuracy, a percentage, a quantity, and so forth. And finally, an objective should make clear any relevant conditions that could affect the learner's capability to perform in the examination situation. What references, tools, and the like that will be provided or denied should be made clear.

Developing Instructional Strategies

Ideally, the teacher should have a wide range of options and resources from which to select in terms of different media, materials, methods, and facilities he can use to achieve the objectives he has set. In real situations, however, there are several factors that tend to limit the amount of flexibility he has. The resources of most schools are quite limited in relation to the media that are now available. Inasmuch as most teachers are in the position of having to work from an adopted textbook, their approach to teaching will undoubtedly be shaped by that particular textbook. Also, when the teacher does elect to use some other medium in the classroom, he typically does not select the medium but, rather, he selects a particular teaching instrument. For example, the motion picture film is one of the most popular audiovisual media used by teachers. But films are not generally made as the result of a decision that motion is a necessary attribute of the materials to be presented. Film makers usually attempt to produce a wide variety of films covering many areas of school curricula. Thus, when choosing an existing piece of material, teachers often make a choice that is different from the one they would have made if they were producing the materials themselves. The form of the material is not important, however, so long as it provides adequate opportunity for learning the content. Many pieces of materials fail to meet this criteria, however, because they present too much information in a short time and provide no satisfactory way for the learner to practice the behavior to be learned.

The teacher of today has an extensive array of educational media from which to choose. Previously, it had been customary to refer to all media other than the textbook as "audiovisual aids." The term "aids" is an unfortunate one in that it gives the impression that some materials, and the techniques that go with them, are standard while others are supplementary or optional. The modern teacher should not be influenced by this false impression. Audiovisual media materials are not "aids;" they are simply part of the array of available media. Their use should not be thought of as something special, a retreat from the routine. The characteristics of each medium suggest the type of teaching tasks for which it is appropriate. Developing instructional strategies is largely a job of matching the right medium and method with particular educational tasks or objectives.

Another factor that will influence a teacher's method of developing plans for utilizing media is his orientation in reference to the learning theories explained earlier. For example, we might consider a unit in elementary social studies on the settlement of the American West. A teacher with a "stimulus" orientation might select a film that dramatizes the difficulty of frontier life by depicting the monotony and isolation of living and showing types of housing, clothing, transportation, work, and so forth. A teacher with a "behavioral" orientation might reject the same film because he feels that it would not contribute significantly to an increase in relevant behavioral competence even though it contains interesting visual and verbal stimuli. The behaviorist would be concerned with identifying the type of evidence that could logically be accepted as proof that a young learner has developed his appreciation of the nature of frontier life. Thus the teacher might turn to a more participatory activity such as a pupil dramatization or a simulation. Or if he does use the film, he might use it in a different way, such as by requiring the children to make specific behavioral responses *during* the showing, even if it necessitates some starting and stopping of the projector. In any event, the behaviorist's orientation is to require participation of *all* pupils in the practice of "terminal behavior," and this is quite different from the typical "stimulus oriented" approach of show-discuss-test.

So many available educational media instruments will present a dilemma for the teacher. He wants to use media that are interesting and motivating but which can be analyzed to some degree in terms of their contribution to learning. Most of the commercial films and related media seem to have been produced by message oriented people and generally do not provide for the type of learner participation which is essential to learning. And so teachers must select films and other media of worth in terms of content and artistic presentation and then devise for themselves a pattern of utilization that will ensure that pupils achieve the desired learning. For the teacher, moving in the direction of clarifying objectives and measuring the outcomes of learning episodes is a never-ending process.

The range of types of educational tasks or objectives that is encountered in the school curriculum is wide, indeed. And, of course, theorists differ as to exactly what these types are. To list and analyze the principal learning objectives is important, not just for the sake of having a classification, but also because this procedure enables one to plan for instructional techniques most appropriate for the type of learning at hand. The following eight types of learning objectives would seem to include almost all learning that takes place in schools: learning factual information; visual identifications; concepts; principles; sequential procedures; psychomotor skills; problem solving; and attitudes and values. Each of these types will be explained shortly and then analyzed in terms of appropriate media application.

The principal media forms that a teacher might use include book media, audio media, still projection media, motion pictures, television, realia, visual displays and exhibits, and teacher presentations. Actually, a teacher presentation can take a variety of forms and can be offered in conjunction with other media; and so it is, strictly speaking, inaccurate to refer to it as a media form. However, since the teacher will be involved in decisions either to "use himself" or to use another medium, it is convenient to think of his presentations in this light.

PRINCIPAL TYPES OF LEARNING ACTIVITIES.   There are a great many different experiences that can lead children to learning. It appears that these can be grouped into four principal types of activities: *exposition, participation, interaction,* and *evaluation.*

1. *Exposition.* So that learning can take place, the learner must undergo some perceptual experience; he must receive information in some form of stimuli. The most common forms of exposition are lectures, reading assignments, media presentations, real life experiences (including traveling, field trips, and so forth), and viewing displays and exhibits. The range of media presently available now provides tremendous flexibility in achieving this function.

2. *Participation.* A very significant element of contemporary thinking in the area of learning theory is that learners should be involved in the learning process; they should be able to respond to stimuli they perceive and then practice the behavior to be learned. This is advantageous to the learner in that responding and participating tend to compel him to learn as the lesson progresses, and it is advantageous to the teacher in that overt practice provides an observable indicator to him that desired learning is taking place. Covert participation or "mental practice" has also been shown to be effective for some types of learning, but the problem here is that there is no sure way for the teacher to ascertain that such practice is taking place. Learner participation can take many forms: outlining and note taking, writing, filling in blanks in programmed sequences, reporting, demonstrating, experiment-

ing, dramatizing, constructing, singing, dancing, and various kinds of work simulation. The most suitable form must be determined for individual learning objectives. This is a very important part of developing instructional strategies.

3. *Interaction.* Perhaps no concept is so dear to the hearts of American educators as the feeling that schools, at any level, must provide ample opportunity for "give and take" between teachers and pupils and between pupils and pupils. It is difficult to describe in very specific terms just what interaction contributes to the learning process, except that it seems to be taken for granted that children must have an opportunity to ask questions, to participate in discussions, to serve on panels or otherwise take part in unstructured, two-way dialogue. Such sessions seem to be quite valuable to pupils in that they present the opportunity not only of having their difficulties explained, but also of expressing their opinions and making comments. The sessions are also valuable to teachers in that they provide sources of feedback on the effectiveness of their teaching, as well as opportunities to evaluate the progress of individual learners. Such interaction usually takes place in small group discussions or seminars, individual conferences, project reports, and simulation sessions. Planning these sessions is also an important part of instructional strategy development.

4. *Evaluation.* Obtaining reliable and comprehensive evaluation of the outcomes of classroom learning experiences is always one of the teacher's most difficult problems. Measuring the effects of media presentations is possibly more difficult because of the added dimensions of communication of materials like films and videotapes. Measuring verbal retention is relatively straightforward, but measuring the effects on a pupil's attitudes and values of a controversial documentary film is not so simple. A more detailed discussion of evaluation will be presented later in this chapter.

STRATEGIES FOR DIFFERENT TYPES OF LEARNING. The principal task involved in developing instructional strategies is relating the best combination of media and method to the particular type of objective at hand. Therefore, it will be convenient to treat each of the eight types of learning discussed in terms of the suitability of various media to foster learning by providing for stimulus exposition and learner participation.

1. *Learning Factual Information.* This, of course, is a very broad category and includes the learning of definitions, nomenclature, names, events, dates, and other types of facts. Because this category is so broad, it is difficult to make specific statements about the best media form to use. Important considerations are that learning large numbers

of facts requires a substantial amount of time, and that pupils learn facts at different rates. Consequently, textbooks and programmed texts are valuable because they allow pupils to proceed at their own pace, while providing unlimited repetition or referring back to material previously covered. Audio media such as films, television, and audiotapes can be useful in teaching facts, but because they move at a preset rate and last for a fixed time, they do not provide well for the varied amount of practice that learners at different levels will need. The visual aspects of film or television may add interest, but the research evidence suggests that they do not add to learning efficiency when the facts to be learned are not actually visual in nature. Visual displays and exhibits, demonstrations, and realia tend to be low in quantity of information presented and thus would be of little use in the actual learning of large amounts of factual information.

2. *Learning Visual Identifications.* This type of learning involves responding to different visual stimuli and developing the ability to discriminate between different visual objects or symbols on the basis of visual characteristics. It is a very common type of learning. Consider the young boy who can name virtually every make and model of automobile on the road today, even though many differ only slightly in terms of exterior trimming. And of course, young girls develop phenomenal powers in this area as evidenced by their ability to identify real mink, last year's hat style, and so forth. Visual identifications learning is important in a number of subject areas including biology, geology, art, geography, dance, industrial arts, and others.

It is to be expected that visual identifications can best be learned through media that realistically depict the relevant visual stimuli with a high degree of definition. Therefore, motion pictures and slides would generally be quite appropriate. Slides may have an advantage over films in some applications because they allow the pace of the presentation to be controlled by the teacher. Films may have an advantage, however, if motion is a relevant attribute of the discrimination to be learned. Television suffers from an inherently lower definition picture, absence of color in monochrome systems, and uncertainty in obtaining exact critical hues and tints in color systems. Realia and visual displays may be effective if the number of visual identifications to be learned is small. The number of highly illustrated reference books of various types is increasing steadily and these books, if available in sufficient numbers in a school, should prove to be quite valuable for visual learning as they have high definition photography and can be studied without time limitations.

3. *Concept Learning.* Concept learning is also very common in human learners and involves the ability to identify phenomena as mem-

bers of a class and to discriminate between that class and other classes. When a child has learned a concept, he can discriminate between *new* instances and non-instances, not used in the teaching sequences. Concepts may have concrete referents, such as *ball, dog,* and *chair.* But they may be much more abstract, such as *electricity, intuition,* and *credibility gap.* Consequently, it is difficult to generalize about employing media in concept learning. Concepts that have direct, physical referents are likely to benefit from still projections using slides and filmstrips. Abstract concepts, like *inflation, assets,* and *productivity,* might be better taught with graphic support in the form of charts and graphs rather than with realistic pictures. And some concepts, like *momentum* and *elasticity,* are most effectively taught with motion pictures. Therefore, media decisions in concept learning must depend upon the critical attributes of the concept and the capabilities of particular media to present them to the learner. If constant interaction between teacher and pupil is desired, as it frequently is in concept learning, then media that the teacher can control, such as still pictures and slides, are most appropriate.

4. *Learning Principles.* Principles involve relationships between concepts. They frequently have an "If A . . ., then B . . ." form. Some principles are expressed as laws or rules, for example, "the most economical shape for a house is rectangular." And some principles have a strategic quality such as "on third down and long yardage, throw a pass." A person who did not understand the basic concepts of football, which include "third down," "long yardage," and "pass," would be almost incapable of learning the principle in a meaningful way. It can be seen that principles are chains of concepts; and so a prerequisite to learning a principle is having a knowledge of the component concepts.

There are several important steps in the teaching of principles. The learner should be informed as to the behavior that will be accepted as an indication that the principle is understood. He should be questioned in a way that ensures that he has knowledge of the component concepts. The learner should be exposed to the principle in a way that enables him to make the proper association between the concepts. And he should be required to demonstrate mastery of the principle, preferably in a realistic or a simulated situation.

It should be clear by now that as learning becomes more complex, the stimulus conditions suitable for achieving learning also become more complex and less predictable. Thus specific media decisions can best be made in relation to a determination of the nature of specific concepts and principles that are to be learned.

5. *Learning Sequential Procedures.* This task involves learning to carry out the various steps of some operation in proper order. The nature of the task could be any one of quite a variety, such as account-

ing, performing an experiment, or assembling a device of some kind. A live demonstration would be one good way to teach procedures; and motion pictures would be another because they provide great flexibility in the selection of camera shots. For procedures that are somewhat complex, the use of a programmed text or manual would seem to be an excellent choice.

6. *Learning Psychomotor Skills.* Learning psychomotor skills usually involves learning a sequence of steps, but with the added constraint of acting with a high degree of accuracy or precision in some manipulative sense. Such learning skills would be quite common in art, sports, engineering, industrial arts, and medicine. This type of learning requires that the child have ample opportunity to practice the skills, and so a live demonstration is useful as are motion pictures. Motion pictures, however, must provide time for learner practice and so they should include places for stopping and practicing. Such motion pictures should also move at a very slow pace so that the learner will have time to look away and locate objects or similar elements of the task without missing something of the film.

7. *Learning Problem Solving.* Problem solving involves applying two or more previously learned principles to a single problem. Research has shown that it is not a good idea to demonstrate the solution to a problem until the learner can recall the steps. It is better to present the learner with the problem, give him instructions as to the nature of the task, perhaps provide some guiding cues, and then let him attempt to solve the problem.

If the problem is of such a nature that all the elements can be provided the learner directly, he might not need any media support other than the teacher's verbal instructions. Media could be very useful, however, in presenting problems to an entire class, problems which they might solve individually or in small groups. This presumes, of course, that the solution to the problem can be described in verbal terms or by simple drawings. Motion pictures and television seem to be most appropriate for presenting problems which might include equipment or people as movable elements. However, many problems can be presented on locally produced paper handouts run off on a duplicating machine.

Discovery seems to be a fundamental element in problem solving, that is, using known principles to arrive at higher level principles. Thus, whether the teacher is using media or making the presentation himself, the trick in teaching problem solving is for the teacher to give enough prompting, but without "tipping off" the solution, so that the learner will recall relevant principles.

8. *Developing Attitudes and Values.* Young people acquire attitudes and values from a variety of sources: their parents, their school, their classmates, their religious affiliation, their neighborhood environment, and the mass media. To change or alter attitudes is not easy. Most people tend to respond to communications that reinforce their present views. They also tend to attach great credence to opinion leaders whether such faith is warranted or not.

From the teacher's point of view, the establishment of a specific objective in terms of an attitude change and then devising a strategy that is reasonably sure of bringing about that change is probably the least certain of all the types of learning he will attempt. Still, this is an area that cannot be neglected just because it is difficult or uncertain. It seems natural to look to the motion picture as a powerful vehicle for communication in this area because it can more realistically dramatize phenomena that are relevant to changing attitudes. Such realities as the fruition of creative discovery, the horror of war, the despair of poverty, and others can be portrayed "in living color" and in a high degree of definition. Probably no other medium produces an equivalent sense of the viewer's identification with the characters on the screen. Picture stories, which appear in some popular magazines, also seem to be quite effective in developing motivations and in altering values.

Implementing Instruction with Media

The use of media in the classroom is no longer a rare occurrence. The principles for utilizing media can be derived from a general consideration of the techniques that make for good teaching in any situation.

First, the learner should be informed as to what he is to learn from the media presentation. He should be introduced to new terms or new concepts before the presentation. It should be remembered that it is very difficult for the average child to master the content of a media program in one showing. It is often difficult for teachers to appreciate this fact since they are already so familiar with the material. Therefore, careful introduction of a program is important. When showing a film, for example, the teacher should make some provision for allowing the learner time to absorb the material. One way would be to stop the film at certain points and discuss or practice certain items. Another would be to show the film once, discuss it, and then show it again to resolve certain questions. As has been demonstrated by television, the "instant replay" is a very valuable technique.

If the film has been used as a springboard into a unit of work, then a variety of follow-up activities may be undertaken by pupils, either individually or in small groups. If the film, or other media presentation, is a segment of the instruction for which definite learning results are expected, then such learning can be tested directly. In any case, the biggest pitfall for the teacher is simply to show the presentation and then to assume that learning has taken place. It is vital that the learner be involved in participation of some form to ensure that he is acquiring the desired competencies.

Evaluating Learning from Media

It is not the authors' intent to deal with testing techniques in this book, but a brief discussion of evaluation problems attendant to media utilization is appropriate. A common fault in such evaluation is the failure to make any attempt to identify and measure learning to be gained from the visual portion of a presentation. An entire course may be built around a sophisticated multimedia presentation system and then, at examination time, the pupil is given a totally verbal, multiple choice examination. The assertion sometimes made by teachers that, "without the visuals, the youngsters would not *really understand* the content" is, scientifically speaking, on a par with witchcraft and old wive's tales. Naturally, it is more difficult to measure the learning to be gained from a picture than that gained from a verbal statement. But this does not mean that attempts to identify and measure such learning should be ignored. Learning from visuals can be tested in two ways, either by requiring verbal descriptions of visual stimuli, or by displaying the visuals during the testing situation and requiring learners to make discriminations or identifications. The latter technique requires that the media materials be available both in the teaching situation and in the testing situation, which suggests, particularly in the case of rented materials, that in the time sequence, evaluation should follow closely behind teaching. This is a good practice, however, since it gives the teacher an opportunity to measure the effects of the media before it is returned to the film library or to whatever source it came from.

In all teaching, it is important to identify objectives, and when media presentations are being used, this is especially true. A learner studying from a textbook can generally figure out what the essential material is and what the teacher is likely to test him on. However, let us consider a film that demonstrates some sequential procedure. The viewing pupil will be asking himself: "Is this just to give me a general idea of what this procedure is all about? Will I be expected to list the steps in the procedure? Or will I be expected to do the work myself?" Obviously, the dimensions of the learning tasks suggested by these three questions are extremely different, and yet we often find such demonstration media being used without any consideration of the level of outcome expected of the learner.

This is not meant to imply that it is easy to identify the learning that visual media affect. Such learning could be very complex. Good media presentations should not be overlooked simply because the teacher does not have the time to define objectives to the Nth degree. It is suggested instead that the teacher be constantly alert to the problem and that he seek to provide increasingly clear descriptions of the desired outcomes of media that he uses repeatedly in his classes.

In discussions of measurement instruments, it has been customary to describe test items in terms of their form—that is, true-false, multiple-choice, essay, and so forth. Actually, a more useful classification is one made according to the basic behavioral process involved in completing the item. The classification suggested here contains four types: *discrimination questions* which require the learner to select from options provided and which include true-false, multiple choice, and matching; *locate* or *recognize questions* which require more complex behavior such as locating parts or identifying features of visual displays, photographs, or similar stimuli; *recall questions* which are short answer-completion or fill-in-the-blanks types; and *constructed response items* which include definitions, explanations, expository statements, drawings, and the like. instructional events, can be set forth.

The elements of a sound evaluation program are, of course, related to the specified educational objectives since the purpose of evaluation is to confirm that objectives have been achieved. The purpose of developing evaluation instruments is to measure learner competency in relation to established criteria, not in relation to other learners. Therefore, the following general requirements for test items can be set forth:

Test items should be based on a clear definition of instructional objectives.

Test items must present conditions which require and elicit behavior at the same level as prescribed in the objectives.

Test items must accurately record the performance the pupil makes.

Test items should seek to elicit behavior that can readily be gauged as either adequate or inadequate.

The teacher who follows the suggestions made here for preparing objectives and test items should find the planning and implementing of instruction to be both easier and more effective.

Summary: Some Criteria of Quality Instruction

Education is a very large enterprise in the United States and a great deal has been written about it. And yet it is hard to find anyone who is bold enough to set forth a definition of "teaching" or to list the criteria by which good teaching is to be recognized. The authors of this book are not so presumptuous as to claim that this will now be done. However, from the foregoing discussion, it should be clear that a number of desirable criteria of good teaching, or of sound mediated instructional events, can be set forth.

1. A clear description of the desired learning outcomes in order to ensure uniform interpretation of objectives among teachers and pupils.

2. The structuring of an instructional program that provides all necessary conditions and stimuli for learning and that accounts for all objectives and sub-objectives in proper sequence.

3. A method of involving children in the learning process so that desired competencies are actually practiced, thus making learner progress orderly, efficient, and observable.

4. A method that provides regular feedback to the pupil as to the correctness of his responses or the adequacy of his competence.

5. A method of adapting instruction to learner capabilities and learning rates.

6. An examination program that accurately and reliably evaluates learner competence at the same level as it was prescribed in statements of objectives.

Good teachers undoubtedly apply techniques that are intuitive and artistic and perhaps unique to their own personalities. All teachers can improve their instruction by employing an empirical approach to some degree or other. This means that if a teacher is actively seeking to incorporate the above characteristics into his instruction, he should devise means of measuring for himself how well he is succeeding so that he will know what should be revised. This continuous try-out and revision is the essence of developing empirically sound instructional events, regardless of the media or method involved.

Such deliberate attention to improving the pupil's cognitive learning should also enhance his acquisition of the higher-level outcomes of teaching, particularly in attitudes and feelings. When a pupil knows clearly what is expected of him, how well he is doing, and where to get individual help, he is likely to increase his approach tendencies towards school and the subject matter. It is in these areas that the teacher is most significantly rewarded: the marginal pupil who does not drop out, and the average pupil who catches on and develops a life-long vocational or personal interest in the subject taught.

4

Still Projection Media

Overhead Projection

In many schools, the most apparent sign of the impact of new educational media is the overhead projector in the front of the classroom. In less than a single decade—only a long summer's day in the rate of adoption of educational innovations—this remarkable device has developed from novelty to necessity in thousands of schools. The initial wondering question of the teacher, "How can I use this strange-looking apparatus?" has given way to the appreciative, "How could I get along without it!"

Teachers find the overhead projector ideal for myriad classroom uses, and with good reason. The overhead projector is the only audiovisual device which was specifically designed for instruction and not adapted from entertainment, scientific, or hobby purposes.

In terms of what it does, the overhead projector throws a large, bright image onto a screen in the front of the classroom, either in direct center or off to one side. The visual information to be projected is contained on transparent material placed on the flat lens-top surface (or stage) of the projector. The bright lamp located beneath the stage transmits light through the transparency into a mirror and lens system (the head) located directly over the center of the stage, and from there is projected onto the screen. Because the transparency is relatively large, up to ten by ten inches, a large amount of light carries the image to the screen, making it fully visible in a normally lighted classroom.

The placement of the projector and the image make overhead projection especially convenient for the teacher to face the class while using the device. From this position, the teacher can talk directly with pupils while pointing out special aspects of the visual, changing transparencies, or even adding information by writing on the transparency with a water-soluble, colored or opaque marker pen.

Facing the class, the teacher can correct student composition exercises or present verbal or graphic support for a lesson by writing directly on an acetate sheet on the stage of the overhead projector.

After primary information is presented on the basic transparency, additional features can be added or subtracted by the flip of a wrist through a series of overlays. The image is being projected on the chalkboard behind the teacher.

Often, the teacher uses the overhead projector as an "electric chalk-board," for, while the class is present, he can write or draw on the transparent surface, which may be either a sheet or a continuous roll of acetate. But one striking advantage of the overhead projector is that the transparencies can be prepared ahead of time and projected instantaneously, eliminating the need to do extensive writing or elaborate drawing on the board while the class is watching and waiting. Sometimes, however, it is important that pupils see certain parts of the drawing or diagram developed *in process*. In such cases, a partially finished transparency can be prepared beforehand and completed in class during projection by adding lines to a graph, figures in a problem, or labels on a diagram.

Because the overhead projectuals are transparent, one can be placed on top of another to add information to a visual. By means of overlays, a visual presentation can be built up in steps. The overlays are attached to a basic mounted transparency and laid over when needed. For example, a teacher may start with the basic outline of an insect, and by successive overlays, add detail and labels. Or in music, the teacher may start with the projected staff and add notes and other musical markings.

Most publishers of instructional materials make available ready-made transparencies which are designed and tested for specific lessons. Often these transparencies are correlated with textbooks and sometimes form the heart of a packaged unit consisting of all the materials a teacher needs to conduct a lesson presentation. There are advantages in using ready-made transparencies, namely, the unusual degree of accuracy in their content and artistic skill in their design, and the preparation time that they save the teacher. Commercially produced transparencies are sometimes packaged in specially designed containers in order to facilitate easy handling of the number needed for a particular lesson. The prices of commercially produced transparencies are continually coming down as volume production and distribution tend to lower costs. In addition, correlated multicolor transparencies and spirit duplication masters help the teacher both in displaying lesson materials and in providing accurate copies for individual pupils.

Teacher-Made Transparencies

The overhead projector would not be so popular, however, if it were not easy for the classroom teacher to make his own transparencies. There are three common methods:

By the *thermal process*, a transparency can be made in less than half a minute by placing a sheet of special transparency film over the selected

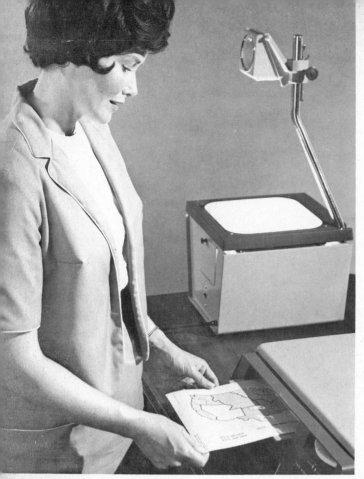

Teacher-Prepared Overhead Transparencies

An overhead transparency is prepared in five seconds by placing a sheet of film over a printed master and running both through the thermal copier.

Visual Products Division, 3M Company

Close-up view of transparency of H_2O cycle in the making.

Visual Products Division, 3M Company

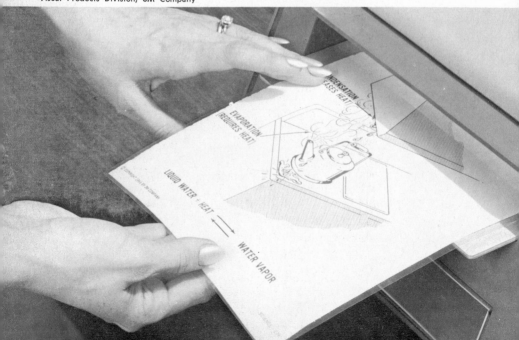

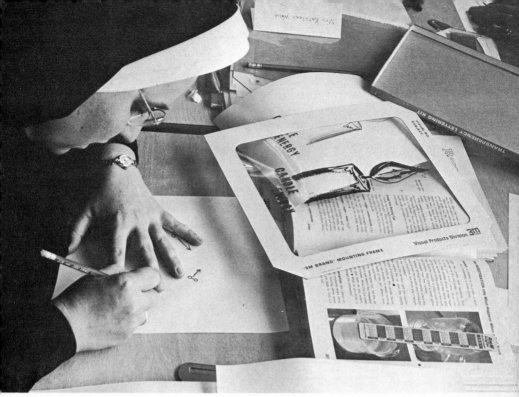

A teacher prepares original material for an overlay, which will be used with a transparency depicting heat energy given off by a candle.

UICC

Selecting a vellum master from a prepared subject master collection, the teacher makes a multiple-overlay color series of transparencies using the diazo method.

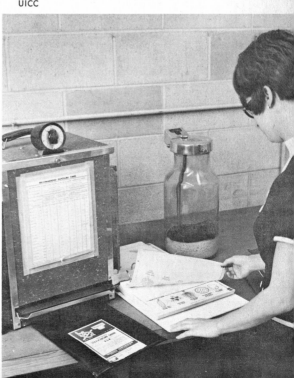

material and running both through a thermal copy machine. The actual run-through takes less than ten seconds. The graphic material to be copied must be printed or written with a carbon-based ink (but most newspapers and typewritten mimeographed materials are). Pupil themes and drawings done in pencil make excellent transparencies. The resulting transparency is the same size as the original. Special film sheets reproduce the material in color (one color per film), and by means of special marking pens and pencils, color can be added to the finished transparency. Other variations on transparency-making by the thermal process are available.

A more elaborate method of making transparencies is the *diazo process*. The visual is first worked out on a sheet of translucent paper (vellum). Various headliner machines produce on transparent film lettering that is excellent for affixing to the vellum. Drawings can be made in black ink or pencil. A number of publishers produce volumes of vellum masters for in-school making of diazo transparencies, and the teacher selects for processing only those needed. The vellum is placed under a sheet of special film of the indicated color and exposed to intense light in an exposure box for a specified number of seconds. When the film and the vellum master are removed from the exposure box, no distinct image can be seen on the film. But when it is placed in an ammonia jar or an ammonia-type blueprint-making machine, the image appears in the preselected color. It is then ready for mounting in a frame. Overlays can be made in different colors to complete a complex transparency.

The *photographic method* of transparency-making uses a camera to photograph the material desired for the projectual. The orthographic "high contrast" film from the camera is developed, the resulting negative is examined, and all undesired information or blemishes are covered with a special opaque fluid. The negative is then placed in an enlarger and printed onto orthographic positive transparency film which is the same size as the stage of the overhead projector. When developed, the transparency can be mounted in the usual way. The photographic method allows a small picture to be enlarged while being converted into an overhead transparency, and it affords high contrast and excellent detail. Drawbacks to this process for ordinary school use are that it requires a photographic darkroom and expends more time and money than the other two methods.

Even with no equipment to produce transparencies according to the three processes described above, the teacher has one even more basic method, and that is working directly with a sheet of acetate. Diagrams can be drawn freehand, or they can be traced with the marking instruments. Cellophane or adhesive sheets can be affixed to provide color. Special contact sheets actually remove illustrations from clay-based paper, such as found in quality magazines, in a form that can be shown on an overhead projector.

Classroom Utilization

Ingenious teachers have also discovered how to substitute plastic wrap for regular acetate sheets. Opaque objects or cutouts can be placed on the transparency stage to cast information in silhouette onto the screen; for example, a magnetic field can be clearly shown by sprinkling iron filings on a glass sheet placed over a magnet on the stage of the overhead projector. Transparent colored circles, jacks, gummed stars, and so forth can be manipulated on the stage of the overhead projector to present a vivid demonstration of unison, junction, and independent sets. In chemistry, a special attachment to the overhead projector allows test tubes filled with transparent fluids to be projected in full color onto the screen. Other transparent plastic models also work. Special transparencies incorporating stressed plastic into the visual patterns can be used on an overhead projector containing a spinning Polaroid disc, and the projected image will appear to be in motion to show direction on flow diagrams or other process charts.

The same art work used to prepare the overhead projection transparency can readily be used to serve as the master for preparing spirit process or offset handouts for pupils. In this way, the youngsters can attend to the projected diagram or drawing and not have to copy it *in toto* into their notes with resulting loss of accuracy and class time. Pertinent labels, notes, and comments can be added instead during the teacher's presentation or during class discussion.

Opaque Projection

Overhead projection is sometimes confused with *opaque projection,* a totally different process for displaying visual information to classes. Opaque projection is a much older method, and may bring reminiscences of hot, bulky, and blinding (when opened to insert material) "black Marias" that used to project student themes, magazine pictures, and seashells. Because of these necessary, but undesirable, viewing conditions resulting from bouncing light off opaque objects rather than from transmitting light through transparent ones, as in overhead projection, the opaque projector seems to be going the way of the hornbook. However, it is premature to write the opaque projector entirely out of the inventory of modern educational media. For preparing graphic materials and displays, the opaque projector can readily enlarge a drawing or map so that the projected image can be traced on the wall, a poster board, or the chalkboard. Exact size can be varied easily by changing equipment position. And it is possible to show full color pictures and objects without intermediate preparation if the teaching situation can accept the necessary nearly total darkness. While intermediate preparation becomes increasingly easy, as shown in the next section, the answer to this instructional problem may lie in selection of a different medium.

Charles Besler Company

Children's color drawings are displayed for an entire class by means of a new higher-output opaque projector.

Slides

The popular image of the vacationing American invariably includes a 35mm camera slung over the shoulder. While undoubtedly many of the resulting slide shows are aimed at personal enjoyment derived from reliving travel experiences, a good many of the pictures taken by touring teachers do enliven geography and social studies lessons in their classrooms throughout the school year.

The 35mm and the increasingly popular 126 Instamatic color slides are very common forms of presentation support, providing as they do a complete variety of visuals available for handy and convenient use. Size alone provides convenience—the 35mm designation refers to the width of the film, although mounted in a 2″ x 2″ mount. Hundreds can be stored in a single tray in a desk drawer. When they are spread out on a glass-topped light table or a sorting stand, the teacher can select a sequence that will best illustrate the narrative. The slides can be loaded in proper order into automatic slide trays, placed in a remote-control slide projector, and advanced or repeated as desired while the teacher carries on an active dialogue with the pupils—asking questions, pointing out items of interest, and showing the visual elements relevant to the lesson.

Once accustomed to taking slides on a trip or field study, the teacher is ready to go into more direct production of instructional slides for classroom use. By means of a copy stand, specially prepared illustrations, portions of books, or three-dimensional objects can be photographed with the 35mm camera. The film can be processed by the local photographic service and returned in slide form. Charts that would be awkward to carry around, or illustrations that are too small to show to a class are easily converted into slides for automatically controlled, bright, full color images on the screen. For best results, the classroom must be at least partially darkened because of the relatively small size of the slide, even though a highly reflective screen is used.

Commercial producers of instructional materials are capitalizing on the popularity and characteristic advantages of slide projection and are marketing sets of slides in a large number of subject areas. In the field of art, a school can obtain nearly all of the world's great painting, sculptural, and architectural masterpieces in color slide form. For social studies, sequential maps and illustrations can be obtained.

Some slides are produced with high contrast information so that they can be projected on the chalkboard instead of on the screen. Then the teacher can write annotations and other pertinent information over the projected image.

By means of the remote-control slide projector, slides can be advanced while the teacher is standing in front of the class. The pictures can be held as long as desired, and can even be backed up to bring a previous image to the screen. Focus problems can be handled by a remote-control mechanism, or in some newer projectors, by a completely

Color Slides: A Versatile and Powerful Teaching Aid

A high school geography teacher selects a particular mountain area of a relief map prior to taking a color slide.

All kinds of pictorial material can be converted into slides with the special copy stand.

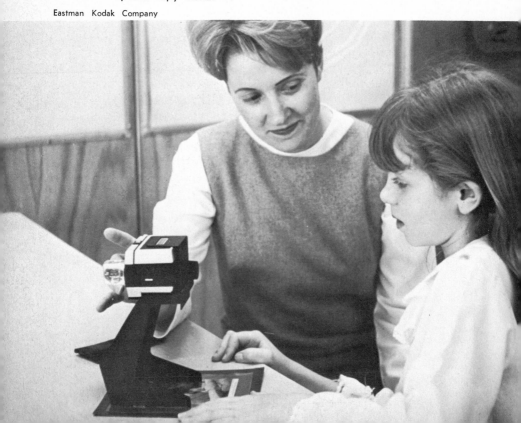

Flash cube illumination is precisely controlled for proper exposure in this pupil made slide.

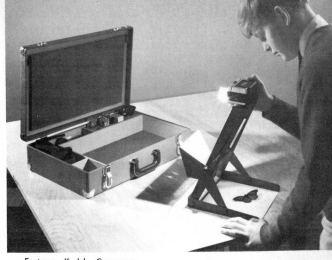

Eastman Kodak Company

Slides are pre-loaded in proper position and sequence in 80-slide trays for remote-control projection.

Eastman Kodak Company

With the daylight screen, ordinary room lighting can be left on during slide presentations.

Graflex Audiovisial Aids, Singer Company

Filmstrips for Group and Individual Use

Classroom filmstrip projectors with automatic features can be remotely controlled for advance, reverse, and focus.

Individualized use of filmstrips is facilitated by small rear projector unit —a major improvement over usual magnifying viewers.

Graflex Audiovisial Aids, Singer Company

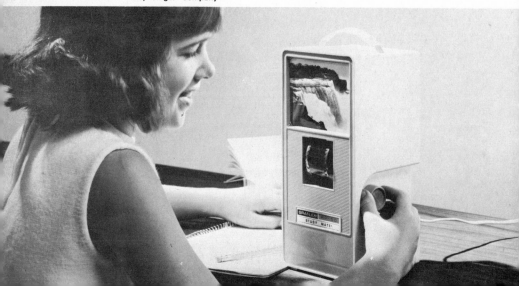

automatic self-focusing device which checks and refocuses each slide as necessary.

Slides taken by the teacher and commercially processed are usually returned in cardboard mounts which are thin and inexpensive. Many schools mount slides in plastic or metal frames between two thin pieces of glass. These kinds of mountings protect the slides and align them consistently in the projector to eliminate many variations in focusing.

While the 2″ x 2″ slide is now the most popular, the 3¼″ x 4″ slide is still being used for special purposes. Its larger size permits more light to pass through the transparent film, and this results in a brighter image on the screen. Various kinds of Polaroid photography have made it possible to make "instant" black and white slides, actually those that can be self-developed in fifteen seconds and then placed in plastic mounts ready for projection. Certain films can be written on directly for a quickly prepared slide, and the same thermal process used in overhead projection can be employed for smaller format transparencies to fit into 3¼″ x 4″ plastic mounts. In addition, there are newer types of 3¼″ x 4″ remote-control projectors.

While the teacher usually talks along with a slide presentation, or engages the class in discussion, he will find that it is easy and practical to record instructions or a prepared commentary to accompany a slide series. When this commentary is put on one track of a stereo tape recorder, signals can be placed on the other track. These signals activate a control device that automatically advances a remote-control slide projector.

Filmstrips

When a slide series, intended for wide distribution in multiple copies, has been completely worked out for instructional effectiveness, it is practical to convert it into a filmstrip presentation. By this process, each slide is photographed and reproduced in approximately one-half size on a single strip of color photographic film. This requires special equipment or the services of a photo-lab. Filmstrips come in small cannisters and are easier to store than slides. Easily loaded into filmstrip projectors, which are sometimes dual-purpose machines with slide handling capability, the frame advance can be controlled manually or automatically.

There are far more filmstrips than slide sets available commercially. One reason is cost. The price of a fifty-frame filmstrip is less than one-fourth the price of a fifty-frame slide set. The fact that the frames in a filmstrip cannot be rearranged whereas rearrangement is easily accomplished with slide sets may occasionally be a drawback to their use.

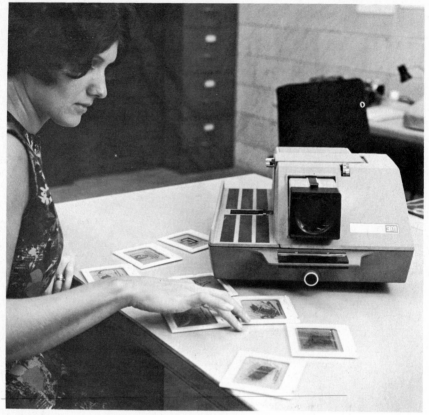

UICC

Large-format (3 1/4 x 4 inches) slides are mounted in interlocking frames for block insertion into automatic, remote-controlled projector. High light output of the large-format slides allows projection in ordinary room light.

Filmstrips can be used by one pupil as well as for class presentations. Individual filmstrip viewers are especially made for this purpose.

More commonly than is the case with slide sets, prepared sound tracks are available to accompany filmstrips. By combining narrative film with sound effects and background music, much relevant instructional material can be presented to pupils at relatively small expense. On automatic sound filmstrip systems employing either phonodiscs or cassette tapes, an inaudible tone advances the filmstrip frames. The mechanics of sound combination are those of audio media which are described in the following chapter.

5

Audio Materials

Most teachers find the phonograph a more familiar piece of audiovisual equipment than any of the others, and thus more convenient and easy to use. Because virtually every teacher owns an operating phonograph of some sort, whether it is called a record player or even a Victrola, the capabilities and mechanics of this device are so well-known that it takes only a little imagination to generate a host of classroom applications.

The best reason for using audio media—of which the phonograph is a prominent but not the sole example—is that sound is necessary for the presentation of a specific subject, or is ideally suited for enhancing interest and understanding in a particular instance. Symphonic music performed by the world's great orchestras is available in the classroom simply by the lowering of a tone arm onto a phonodisc. Dramatic passages in literature and plays come to life when they are read by noted actors. Recorded resource materials for all age groups and curriculum areas are found in abundant variety. There are folk songs, fairy tales, sound effects, academic lectures, military bands, and moments in history. The speeches of political leaders and radio commentators bring back the sounds of events past.

The Phonograph

The audiovisual model of the phonograph designed for classroom use is a rugged model that contains certain features not usually found on home models. Phonographs are produced in both monophonic and stereophonic models. All of the essential sound in a recorded performance is contained in a monophonic version; a spacial dimension for proper perspective and added realism is given in a stereophonic version. In order that full stereophonic reproduction can occur, a stylus in the tone arm of the phonograph must pick up separately each of two sound channels in the groove of the phonodisc and pass into separate speakers placed some distance apart. Monaural records which are still on hand can be played on stereophonic phonographs, but the sound from each speaker will be identical; and similarly, the newer stereo records can be played on monophonic phonographs without excessive stylus wear, although only one of the sound channels will be heard.

Audiotape Recording

Versatility in using audio media comes with the audiotape recorder. Unlike the phonodisc in which the audio information is permanently fixed in the grooves, audiotape has a metallic oxide coating in which magnetic patterns are formed as it passes over the recording head. When the tape passes over the playback head, the information is picked up and processed similarly to the amplification and speaker system in the phonograph. The key distinction is in the impermanence of the information on the audiotape. Since most audiotape machines have both record and playback functions, audiotape can be played scores of times (without appreciable loss of quality or addition of noise as in the phonodisc), then erased and rerecorded as desired.

Thus the audiotape recorder gives the teacher the means to produce custom original or composite instructional audio materials. Audiotape recordings can easily be made by taking the microphone and picking up, for instance, the sounds of the street or marketplace and adding voice commentary. In this way, the aural dimension of a foreign city, as well as the visual, can be brought into the classroom. Special attachments allow radio programs to be recorded directly on tape without the added distortion and quality loss of placing the microphone in front of the radio speaker. Pupils can record their own voices. Interviews with school visitors can be captured and retained. A teacher can make an original sound track for a slide series by speaking extemporaneously or by reading from a prepared script into the recording microphone. Certain passages from phonodiscs can be dubbed onto audiotape to facilitate classroom presentation. While pieces of audiotape can be physically spliced together by means of precise cutting and joining, using a special adhesive tape—and this indeed is the way to mend the tape that occasionally breaks—the best quality composite audiotape materials are made by electronically editing, using two machines.

Audiotape recorders are becoming smaller and easier to use—as indeed they would have to be if a teacher were to carry one around like a camera to record the travel sounds mentioned above. Through the use of transistors and other miniature devices, the size of the audio-tape recorder has shrunk dramatically, so that good quality recordings can be obtained from portable units the size of an attaché case or handbag. Standard classroom audiotape recorders have a speaker large enough—or two speakers, in the case of stereophonic systems—for full-range listening in classroom-size groups.

Operation of an audiotape recorder is easy to learn if a few principles are remembered. Essentially, the tape must come off a supply reel and pass through a guide channel that brings it in contact with the recording and playback heads, and then it must be wound onto the take-up reel. The controls are clearly marked on must machines: speed selection (normally 3¾″ or 7½″ per second, with higher fidelity possible at the faster speed, a factor more critical in music recording than in speech); a play button, fast forward and fast reverse to enable the operator to locate a particular section rapidly; and a record button. The latter requires simultaneous pressing of a special safety catch to prevent the mistake of putting the machine into the record mode when only playback is desired, thus erasing the information on the tape. Volume meters indicate proper recording and playback sound levels.

Higher quality audiotape recordings are possible when a school has a recording studio. One can be set up quite simply by treating acoustically a small room, the recording studio, and installing a large glass window to separate this room from the control room where the actual recording equipment is operated. In this room, the level and quality of the studio sound is monitored; here, also, the studio presentations can be combined with introductory or background music, pre-recorded commentary, or other sound effects.

Utilizing Audio Media

Phonodiscs and audiotapes are similar in that they both make presentations that are of fixed duration and that move at a constant pace and are, therefore, in effect a series of transient stimuli. In contrast, slides, chalkboard presentations, study displays, realia, and the like can be viewed for indefinite periods of time. Motion pictures and television programs, whether broadcast or closed-circuit, also have the fixed rate —fixed duration—transient stimuli characteristics. Consequently, there is a great deal of similarity in the basic principles for utilizing these various media. In this chapter, a fundamental utilization scheme for audio materials is discussed, but the same basic steps can also be applied to the use of films and television.

In using such media, there is no one universal technique that fits all educational situations. However, a five-point procedure that has quite general application to most classroom media usages is suggested here.

UICC

Pupil Interaction with Audiotape Materials

High school pupils in individual carrels listen to foreign language recordings of native speakers, under language laboratory teacher's supervision.

Pupils in intermediate grades match sound and lettered word on the Language-Master ® audiocard system.

Bell and Howell

Bell and Howell

Grade school pupils work independently with Drilltapes practicing math problems to insure concept learning and computation skills.

Teachers are free to help other students when individuals or groups are actively engaged with supplementary teaching tape cassettes, which require worksheet responses.

1. Develop a utilization plan. Preview audio materials, listening to them carefully and critically, and identify the learning outcomes for which they are appropriate. Identify the important terms and concepts contained in the program and make plans to ensure that prerequisite concepts are understood by the pupils. Decide on a presentation technique. You may wish to play the audio materials once and then have a follow-up activity; to play them in segments with activity interspersed; to play them through once and then again with frequent stopping for discussion or practice; or to provide some kind of handout that guides pupil participation. Also, an important part of developing a utilization plan is to decide on test items that will be used to measure learning that results from the listening experience.

2. Prepare the children for listening. Try to stimulate interest in the program by making introductory comments. Explain the program and the reason for using it. You might list key words or concepts on the chalkboard or employ a handout to guide pupil participation. The important thing is that they be given a good idea of what will be expected of them in terms of learning from the listening experience.

3. Play the program. Encourage pupils to listen quietly and carefully. Some method of evoking their participation should be employed, whether the participation is to be overt or implicit. Overt participation might be in the form of taking notes, recording observations, completing statements, or answering questions. Implicit or covert participation can be improved by encouraging the children to concentrate on what they are hearing, to analyze what is being said, to arrange facts or concepts in their minds, to react to different points of view, or to devise solutions to problems presented.

4. Engage in follow-up activity. After most media presentations, it is a good idea to have some type of activity to ensure that learning has taken place, to fill in the gaps where the presentation fell short of expectations, to clarify misunderstandings, or to extend the learning to new but related areas. The discussion is a popular form of follow-up, but there are other activities, such as pupil projects, reports, panel discussions, a game or simulation, or a field trip. The presentation and the follow-up activity together should constitute an integrated and total learning experience.

5. Evaluate learning from the listening experience. Evaluation of the outcomes of a media event is really no different than evaluating outcomes of conventional events. The important thing is to confirm that desired learning has taken place and that the teacher's utilization strategy has been effective.

Mincom Division, 3M Company

An elementary teacher records a story for her class.

So far, emphasis has been on the use of audio materials in classroom situations. This is because audiotape recordings have contributed markedly to the individualizing of instruction by making lesson materials available to pupils outside of regular group instruction.

First, the individual machines have become cheaper and easier to operate through the introduction of cartridges or cassettes, which need merely to be slipped into the machine in one piece, eliminating the threading which is necessary on a reel-to-reel machine. In a tape cartridge, the tape is rewound continuously as it is used, but in a cassette, both a supply reel and a take-up reel are encased in a plastic shell that will fit only one way into the machine. Cassettes are capable of fast forward and reverse operation.

Secondly, a different kind of magnetic recording/playback device makes use of the audiocard which is similar in appearance to a data processing card but which contains a magnetic stripe along the lower edge. The audiocard, which is like a flash card with sound, is placed in a slot in the device and is then moved along to the opposite side. Up to fifteen seconds of sound can be played back through a speaker or headphones. In elementary reading, words can be spelled out on the cards, and the sound of the word is contained on the magnetic stripe. Similarly, the process applies to the sounds of letters, phonic symbols, and foreign vocabulary, using pictures as well as words for visual stimuli.

Thirdly, listening stations can provide individual access to audio information sources without direct pupil manipulation of the materials or machines. The pupil has an access device, either a dial or a touch-tone panel, and a headset. The information sources are contained in a bank of audiotape recorders which are activated by signals from pupil stations and which then send programs out in response. The most common application of this arrangement is the *language laboratory*, in which a pupil can hear the sound of the language he is learning. In some language laboratories, several languages and lessons can be available simultaneously, and the pupil either is assigned to one or he may choose one. Two kinds of audiotape recording units are used in the language laboratory: the *audio-passive*, in which the pupil hears the lesson presentation and follows instructions by himself if oral response is indicated; and the *audio-active*, in which the pupil records on his own track as he repeats phrases, answers questions, or produces phonic elements as directed by the voice on the primary track. The language laboratory teacher or attendant can monitor the pupil's responses during the presentation to any station, and the pupil can play back his own recording for comparison with the model. By means of the language laboratory, the pupil can hear a native speaker of the language at the same time that he is studying written texts and workbooks. By special adaptations, oral tests can be given to the class, with only the individual responses recorded for each child, allowing the teacher to check them very quickly for grading.

The language laboratory type of arrangement can be used for commercial education courses, such as typing and shorthand, as well as for music, speech, and other subjects.

Performance Analysis

Whether in the language laboratory or in the classroom, an audio-tape recording can give a pupil an idea of the sound of his oral performance. Many persons find it difficult at first to recognize their own

Audiotape Instructions in the Laboratory

A student at Hamline University learns the proper procedure for operating an infrared spectrophotometer by listening to step-by-step instructions recorded on an audiotape cassette.

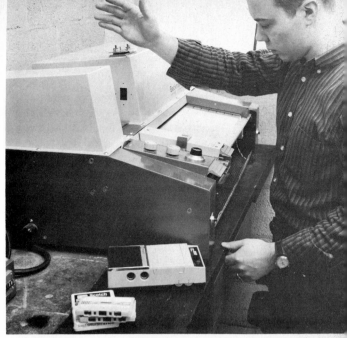

Mincom Division, 3M Company

Placing of the audiotape player in the laboratory enables the individual student to conduct a biology experiment independently.

Mincom Division, 3M Company

Taped programmed laboratory instruction can be supplemented by visuals displayed from the overhead projector.

voices when they listen to an audiotape recording. The reason is that, in speaking ,sound waves pass in many ways from the vocal folds in the larynx to the receptors in the ear, through bone and soft body tissues as well as the air. In the audiotape recording, only the sound that is transmitted through the air is recorded and played back. A teacher sometimes has to reassure a pupil that the sound is indeed his voice as others hear it.

When using the audiotape recorder for speech performance analysis, teacher and pupils should remember that only a part of the communication effectiveness is attributable to voice alone. The audiotape recorder is excellent for shaping voice performance skills, but it is not adequate for self-confrontation with a total public speaking performance. It makes a record of the words and how they are heard; it does not show action and facial expression, and for recording group discussions, it does not show participant reactions as well. When such visual elements are necessary and relevant, using the audiotape recorder alone will sometimes be misleading help. For such situations, the solution is given in a later chapter on video recording.

6

Motion Pictures

For many teachers, the unusual thing about motion pictures in the classroom is that they are no longer unusual. They may remember from their own schooling when having a movie was an exciting and perhaps diversionary event in the stream of ordinary lessons; but the pupil of today regards film as a regular and natural way to acquire information and to participate in visual experiences.

Motion Picture Characteristics and Capabilities

The sound motion picture film is the most powerful single audio-visual presentation medium, as a brief technical explanation will bring out. As anyone unwinding a foot or so of film off a reel can see, a continuous strip of individual pictures (frames) does not produce a motion picture until projected—and then the motion is in the eye of the viewer. But because the film does contain a series of individual pictures, the producer or the user of an instructional motion picture has a variety of techniques and illusions at his command:

1. Individual pictures in a motion sequence can be held on the screen, either by the projectionist's shifting the projector into the "still frame" mode (on projectors so equipped), or by the producer's printing the same frame again and again (freeze frame). Thus, for example, a moment in time can be studied to learn how the wave pattern is formed when an object hits the surface of a liquid.

2. Motion picture film shot at greatly accelerated speed can be shown at normal rate, and the result is "slow motion" as, for instance, a swimming competition dive which can be analyzed for details that occur too fast for the eye to catch.

3. Frames taken at a reduced rate and projected at normal speed produce "fast motion," such as a comic speed-up of automobiles and

57

pedestrians in an impossible mad scramble; but when the frames are taken at regular intervals, a slowly developing phenomenon can be made to complete its action in a short viewing period, such a "time lapse" effect that shows a flower bud bursting into bloom in three seconds.

4. Single frames can be taken as changes are made in the scene or event being filmed, and the "stop motion" effect will animate the changes to appear as live action: puppets can move their bodies and change facial expressions; blobs of clay can grow into fantastic shapes; people and objects can pop in and out of the action.

These effects and techniques are a part of the vocabulary of the motion picture. Pupils are intimately familiar with them from television commercials which show such animated motion as a loaf of bread baking in one puff and candy bars marching around a table. Youngsters always want to know how things are done. Learning from films is aided by knowing how motion picture techniques work, just as learning from books is aided by knowing how paragraphs work.

The motion picture combines the graphic arts with photography. Along with adding titles, labels, captions, or directions to pictures, graphic artists can make series of individually different drawings which when photographed form animated motion. While borrowing the familiar technique of the cartoon, parts of diagrams can be made to move to show processes, such as the cyclic action of the rotary combustion engine.

In addition to images, motion pictures convey simultaneous sound, precisely synchronized with the picture to present dialogue, or to present natural sound of the event shown, such as the roar of a rocket launching or the clop-clop of horses hooves on cobblestones, together with a narrator's voice. Often, appropriate music enhances the cinematographic presentation.

The full color capability of motion picture film allows for the instructional use of *actual color*, that is, the color of actual scenes or objects as photographed, as in the pageantry of the changing of the guard at Buckingham Palace or the subtle color change in chemistry demonstrations of acid testing—and *symbolic color*, in which maps and diagrams contain color-coded information, or demonstration objects such as the popular Cuisenaire rods in mathematics, which are distinguished by colors as well as by length.

Motion Picture Applications in Education

The motion pictures most directly applicable for classroom use are those specifically conceived, produced, and distributed for educational purposes. For almost every area of the curriculum in elementary and secondary schools, there can be located pertinent and useful films, produced and/or sponsored by educational institutions, commercial producers, governmental agencies, religious organizations, and private interest groups. Sources of educational films, along with other outside instructional materials, are found in the Appendix.

The fact that a motion picture is made specifically for instructional purposes in no way diminishes its potential for creative and artistic excellence. Benjamin Britten's famous symphonic work, "Variations and Fugue on a Theme of Purcel," was composed as illustrative score for an educational film entitled *A Young Person's Guide to the Orchestra.* Film festivals regularly bestow awards to educational motion pictures for cinemagraphic achievement.

But the key distinction of an educational motion picture is the process by which it is produced. Ideally, the producing agency should follow the procedures described in Chapter 3. The producing agency might be a unit within an educational institution, particularly a university, or a school system. Commercial companies which are in the business of making educational films ensure the quality, usefulness, and effectiveness of their products by employing professional script writers, directors, cameramen, technicians, and editors to work with educational consultants who are subject matter and teaching experts. Try-outs of films with actual classroom groups is considered an essential part of the development of educational motion pictures.

At the command of the film-making team is an intimate knowledge of the characteristics and capabilities of film. By means of magnifying lenses, the camera can explore the tiniest details of a mechanism or living organism and blow them up in projection to full screen size. People in other cultures and in distant locations can be intimately viewed as if they were being visited. Wherever man can send or take the camera, whether it be to the depths of the ocean or to the surface of the moon, the scene can be recorded for later classroom observation. Events that occurred before the advent of the motion picture camera can be recreated via dramatization so that the pupils can, in mediated fashion, witness the key events in our history; similarly, the foreseeable future can vividly be dramatized. Actual phenomena which, by their very complexity, are difficult to understand clearly are made clear via film animation. Potentially dangerous objects or activities may safely be viewed. The thousands of current titles of educational films attest to their acceptance by teachers as resources for regular use.

Classroom Utilization

The procedures for effective utilization of motion pictures have general aspects that apply both to in-class group showings and to out-of-class individual viewing.

Eastman Kodak Company

Motion Pictures in the Classroom

All eyes are on the screen during the showing of a 16mm sound motion picture in geography.

Film loops are incorporated as a regular part of a science class.

Ealing Corporation

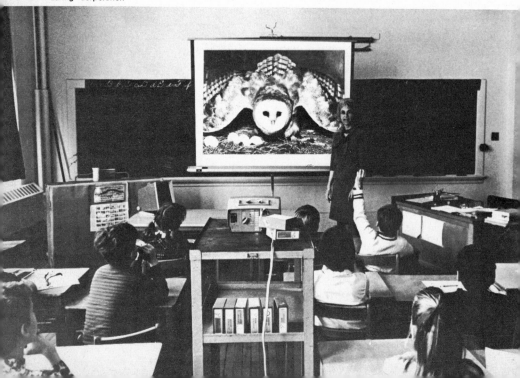

First, the teacher needs to know what materials are available. Chapter 10 provides a more complete discussion of the kind of assistance the media specialists provide in selecting, ordering, and supplying films to teachers. But the key tool for the teacher is the catalog, provided by the school system or other producing or rental agencies, from which he can identify those titles which appear to be most appropriate to the subject and grade. While catalog listings are often sketchy as to the specific content and treatment of the material, film guides might go into more detail are available. These latter describe the objectives of each film, designate the specific school population group for which it was made, give a detailed summary of content, and suggest pre-showing and follow-up activities. Some film guides contain evaluation data on the validation of the use of the film with actual classroom groups.

All too often, however, film guides are available to the teacher only after the film has been selected and ordered. In such situations, the teacher has to rely on the integrity of the catalog and the reputations of the film producer and the distribution agency for proper selection procedures. The resourceful teacher will also get recommendations from other teachers who use films and who may be familiar with acceptable titles. Teachers should keep notes on films that are successful with their classroom groups so that when it is time to re-order, they will know the titles they want. (It is easy to forget a title and difficult to locate a film without it.) These notes should be available to other teachers to help with their selection. Some schools keep a file of film evaluations. Curriculum guides also list motion pictures and other media materials that planners have found pertinent to the support of lesson units. One must trust that the curriculum planners have themselves used and evaluated the films they recommend.

While direct previewing of the film is the best way for the teacher to decide whether to use the film in its entirety, in part, or not at all, in many cases this highly desirable practice is not possible. Film producers generally send out preview prints only to those schools or education agencies that have indicated a possible intent to purchase. Individual schools which borrow or rent normally cannot obtain preview prints for evaluation. When films are owned by the school system itself, previews are more easily arranged without cost during periods when the film is not in demand for classroom use; however, lack of time prevents many teachers from such utilization of their audiovisual library.

When previewing educational motion pictures, teachers should note content, both in terms of concepts and of examples, vocabulary, presentation techniques, and errors or omissions. In planning for the use

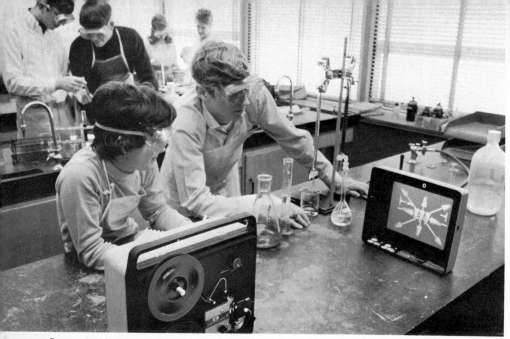

In the science laboratory, the theory underlying chemical reactions is explained by animated film, which can be stopped on a single frame or repeated as needed by the pupils.

High school football players are able to analyze each movement of a play by having the coach point out critical actions in frame-by-frame advance of the motion picture film.

of the film, errors can be corrected and omissions compensated for; thus a hair-trigger rejection mechanism that some teachers activate at their first objection can be stayed until the potential value of the film can be considered in conjunction with all other pre-class and follow-up activities.

Pre-showing activities include logistical arrangements such as ordering the film for the proper day, arranging the room for satisfactory group viewing, and seeing that the projector is in working order and that it is correctly loaded with the film. The classroom, team-teaching room, or regular place of instruction is the best choice of location for viewing the film. Herding several classes into an auditorium, or transferring the class to a special projection room is disruptive and more conducive to inattention. Motion pictures are instructional devices and should normally be a regular, natural part of the usual classroom environment.

Every school has a different balance of duties between those that the teacher performs and those that are provided by media services. Teachers should know the mechanics of film projection so that they can handle the task themselves if necessary. Advances in equipment make the task easier; superior rear-view and daylight screens require minimal room darkening; automatic loading projectors require only four or five simple operations, none of which requires the teacher to thread the film manually through the projection track.

For many teachers, though, the obstacle is not the actual operation of the projector so much as the fear of experiencing difficulty with it while the class is watching. Fortunately, most of the anticipated problems never occur; practice produces confidence, and an increasing use of paraprofessionals, such as classroom aides and audiovisual technicians, will alleviate the situation further and release the teacher for the pre-viewing activities which are specifically instructional.

When getting the class ready for the film, the teacher can create a bridge between previous class experiences and the content of the film, pointing out specific things for which to look and questions for which answers will have to be sought. The previewing serves as a key for guiding the pupils' learning activities. When the teacher knows what the film is about, he is able to discuss the vocabulary and other related matter, and he can help the pupils to become aware of potentially confusing film techniques. If previewing is not possible, even a review of the catalog description may be of some help in preparing the class. During the showing of the film, the teacher should resist any temptation to engage in other chores, for pupils tend to emulate the motivation of the teacher; it is more important that the teacher observe the reactions of the pupils as they watch the film. Even with a sound film, the teacher

Motion Picture Projectors Designed for Easier Use by Teachers

The Bell and Howell Autoload 16mm projector has a self-loading feature that automatically threads the film through the projector.

The Kodak Instamatic projector allows a teacher to record her own sound track on the magnetic stripe of the Super 8 film being projected.

With the Technicolor 1000 projector, a teacher inserts a cartridge containing up to thirty minutes of Super 8 film with an optical track for instant availability of sound motion pictures.

can make comments, stopping the projector occasionally to get pupil responses. While a substantial portion of the information presentation function is assumed by the film media, the classroom teacher remains in command of the situation, controlling the ultimate pace and providing supplementary information. This is essential in some fields, especially if the film is a few years old. A list of follow-up activities is usually contained in the film study guide; these suggested activities include class discussions for recall and extension through additional examples, to theme writing and outside reading. When the film deals with skills training or demonstrations, the follow-up activities should include pupil practice with actual materials.

Demonstration projects have shown that when a wide variety of films is readily available in the school building, or even in special collections for certain grades and classrooms, the utilization of film increases markedly. It is perhaps only a matter of time until the most useful films will be as easily obtainable as are books for the classroom teacher's daily use.

Technical Advances in Format and Equipment

One technological advance that is hastening this day is the introduction of 8mm film in both silent and sound versions. The more recent Super 8 format requires only a little more than one-fourth the amount of film necessary for the standard 16mm, and its picture quality is eminently satisfactory in terms of resolution, color clarity, and brilliance for use in the average size classroom. Not only has the film format helped to increase availability through lowered cost, but the projectors designed for Super 8 are particularly easy to carry, load, and use. In some, special cartridges feed the film directly through the projector onto a specially notched take-up reel, and then rewind it back into the cartridge. In others, a continuous-loop cartridge is plugged into the projector (it will fit one way—the proper one) and a single switch turns the projector on. Films can be changed simply by pulling out the continuous-loop cartridge and plugging in another one. Sound film loop cartridges, with either magnetic or optical tracks, play up to one-half hour.

Besides increasing availability of film for classroom use, the Super 8 projectors and film cartridges extend the patterns of use. Pupils can now have individual access to film materials as they do to books. Some longer 16mm classroom films have a series of related film loops for subsequent individual in-depth study. For example, a 16mm sound classroom film on Eskimos may have complementary film loops showing how Eskimos make the special tools they were seen using in the longer film.

Saga of a Film Loop Series

Students under the direction of Gregory Beckway at Glenbrook North High School, Illinois, construct a large-scale stream table, using colored sands and particles to show effects of water action.

Hubbard Scientific Company

With the stream table completely protected from sun and rain, the natural building processes are filmed in time-lapse, slow motion, and normal speed photography.

Hubbard Scientific Company

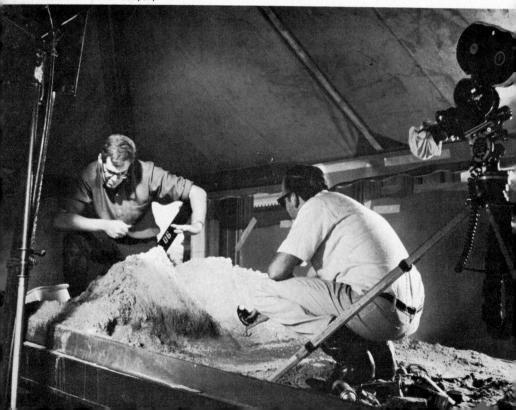

bbard Scientific Company

Delta

Hubbard Scientific Company

Talus Cone

Different geological phenomena are identified and edited into a series of individual film loops, showing formation of deltas, sedimentation, stream development, waterfalls, and others. If it seems hard to understand these phenomena by looking at these small black and white still frames, the point is made for using the motion picture's dynamic portrayal in color and movement.

Hubbard Scientific Company

Cut-Off with Oxbow Lake

bard Scientific Company

Each completed film loop is accompanied by a study guide, presenting key questions requiring predictions relative to each scene, background information, and complete answers.

Ealing Corporation

Small groups or individual pupils insert film loop cartridges into the Technicolor Super 8 projector for detailed study of phenomena in a full-range of scientific topics.

Eastman Kodak Company

Young film makers document their environment with the tools and the language of the visual medium.

Science fiction film of a flight to Mars is made by shooting the interior of a model spacecraft. The picture on the screen in front of the center miniature figure is a rear-projection image from the movie projector in the background.

Eastman Kodak Company

Eastman Kodak Company

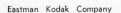

Teen-age John Dentino directs his modern day Alice and her mod, the Mad Hatter, in a scene from his film, "A Jug of Bread, a Loaf of Wine, and Lewis Carroll in a Barrell."

Cartridge-loading automatic-exposure Super 8 film cameras place the film maker's art in the hands of elementary school pupils.

Editing is the key step in film making. Here, 17-year-old Tava Daez of Corvallis, Oregon, works on her award winning film, "Sidewalk."

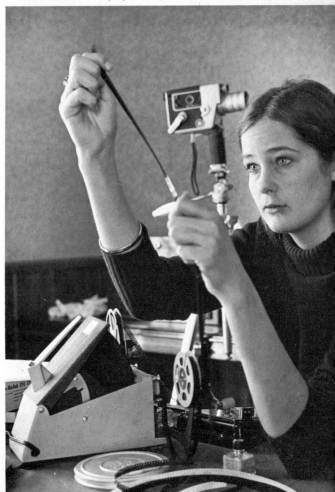

Education about Film

While the most prevalent use of film in elementary and secondary schools is in direct support of instruction in regular subjects, a remarkable growth in instruction about film itself is being experienced at all levels of education. Whether called "film literacy" or "media study," film is becoming curriculum content matter. Such use is a step beyond the showing of feature films or common short subjects for entertainment, diversion, and time filling. Pupils are receptive to the study of the history anid techniques of the film and to the learning of new terminology such as long-shots, dissolves, superimpositions, establishing shots, and jump cuts, while at the same time they study the *way* films communicate. The great films of the past half-century are studied for content and style, comparing idea to execution, and representation to effects. Film study courses build on pupil interests and develop appreciations of the most distinctive twentieth-century art form.

In-School Film Making

From film utilization and film study, the next step is film making. Simplified outfits now enable the teacher to film instructional materials directly, utilizing the self-loading Super 8 film cartridge and automatic film camera with zoom lens. The operation is more than aim and shoot, though, for planning comes first. This must include the determining of the sequence of shots that the pupils need to see in order to learn; it includes setting up these sequences for photography; and finally, it includes editing the processed rolls to determine the proper length of each segment. In this manner, a field trip can be preserved for later presentation to the class, or an instructional series in athletic skills, science experiments, or art techniques can be made for later use by individual pupils. Magnetic striping on the film and special recording/playback projectors provide for the later addition of commentary. Recently developed equipment now permits simultaneous photography and sound recording to get a fully synchronized sound motion picture.

The most dynamic use of film in education occurs when pupils get their hands on cameras and other film-making equipment themselves. Even elementary school pupils can use film for storytelling or artistic image-making. The same youngsters who struggle over writing a composition often display remarkable creativity and industry in working out a complete film, from original idea to final production. The more the pupil has been exposed to film and television programs, the more likely he is to generate strikingly advanced film concepts in his work, sometimes causing the teacher to wonder what is going on in the film, and what it means. In such cases, he can participate in a discussion with the pupils to find out. They know. Film is their language.

7

Television

Television is at once the most heralded and the most tested of all the new media. While it was a self-evident fact from its first appearance that children could learn from television, two decades of research have gone into exploring virtually every possible way that television could affect instruction, administration, and research in our schools.

Most commonly, the research design has compared *conventional* teaching with *television* teaching. In this connection, conventional teaching means what a teacher would ordinarily do in front of a class, and all too often, television teaching means doing the very same thing in front of a television camera. As might be expected, the predominant finding is that the measurement methods employed in the research find no significant difference between the two.

From the standpoint of the classroom teacher, television can be considered either an ally or a rival. As an ally, an instructional television series coming in from outside sources can complement the capabilities and energies of the classroom teacher by providing expertly planned and presented lessons in a wide variety of subjects, especially art, music, science, and foreign languages, with which not every elementary teacher is equally comfortable. But even with an ally, one can be uneasy. The compelling nature of the medium lends special status to the teacher appearing on television, and sometimes overshadows the classroom teacher who is in daily contact with the pupils.

The challenge is to find ways of utilizing television along with the classroom teacher and other resources for best results. With the shifting emphasis in the teacher's role to that of manager of learning instead of presenter of information, the power communication and logistical capabilities of television can be put into their proper context.

Television Comes to the Classroom

Standard television receivers bring in programs broadcast from educational and commercial television stations.

A portable videotape playback unit located in a classroom on the DuBois Campus of the Pennsylvania State University enables students in general engineering to view lessons as determined by the local schedule.

The Electronic Video Recording device further simplifies the distribution and utilization of television materials. Up to 52 minutes of programming can be contained on a seven-inch cartridge of dual-track film which fits into the special EVR player.

C & D CBS Laboratories

In the classroom, the teacher, by pressing a button, can display the program of Robert Frost reading his poetry. An ordinary television receiver is attached to the EVR player.

C & D CBS Laboratories

Television Characteristics and Capabilities

As a medium of communication, television can perform certain functions with ease and effectiveness. Television can *magnify images,* using ordinary lenses to enlarge the plane dimensions of an object by one hundred times, and many more times using microscopic attachments. Television can *multiply images* by displaying the same picture on many screens simultaneously, so that any number of pupils can see a particular presentation. The television screens can be any distance away from the camera, permitting television to *transport images* to where the pupils are throughout a building, a school system, or the nation. The television display can *combine images,* placing two pictures together on a split-screen by adding labels and identifying titles. Finally, television can *store images* by recording on videotape for immediate or delayed playback.

Further, television creates illusions that can assist the communication of instruction. The television set maintains pupil *attention* because the screen is the source of light and the speaker a source of sound. The television teacher creates the illusion of *intimacy* by looking directly into the camera lens, fostering the feeling of direct contact with the viewing pupil. Television conveys a sense of *immediacy,* as if the occurrence were taking place at the given moment. Finally, television achieves *synthesis* by fusing various dispersed events into a related simultaneous whole.

Methods of Television Dissemination

There are some special technical considerations that, while they do not affect the pupil viewing situation, nevertheless influence the availability of televised materials. The teacher should know about them to facilitate dealing with parents and educational planners.

The same televised lessons may come to the classroom in different ways. Regular broadcasting stations radiate television signals either on the VHF band (channels 2-13) or the UHF band (channels 14-84). While the majority of televised lessons (the basic staple of *instructional television,* which is the term commonly used to differentiate such programs from the broader cultural or general educational programming) are transmitted by non-commercial public television stations (formerly known as educational television stations), televised lessons are sometimes carried as part of public service broadcasting by regular commercial television stations. An important point about any broadcast televised lesson is that it is available in the home, on an ordinary television receiver, at the same time that it is received in the schools.

Closed-circuit television refers to any system whereby the routes of transmission are controlled so that the signal cannot be received by outsiders. Most commonly, a high capacity (coaxial) cable carries the television signal throughout a single building or campus complex, and between distant buildings or school systems by either cable or a pin-point transmission beam through the air, known as a micro-wave link. In many areas, cable television systems (CATV) are installed to carry a wide variety of television programs and to provide improved reception in housing areas. Televised lessons may be carried on spare channels of such systems. The point of all closed-circuit systems is that each separate receiving location has to be hooked up to the system.

A somewhat hybrid transmission system, known as the 2500 mega-Hertz system, is used to send televised lessons to restricted geographical areas without the use of wires. This method actually broadcasts a television signal, but only special receiving devices can make use of the signal and convert it to a form that can be seen on ordinary television sets. Sometimes this method is called "broadcast closed circuit" because the signal is radiated through the air, although it functions as a closed reception system. The advantage of 2500 mega-Hertz operations is an overall lower cost than a complete cable system, at the same time that many more 2500 mega-Hertz channels are available than standard broadcasting ones.

Such terms as have just been discussed are frequently used in newspaper articles about instructional television and in conversations in educational circles, and a basic understanding of the differences in transmission systems will provide a more secure base to concentrate on the area that most concerns the classroom teacher, that of using the lesson once it arrives in the classroom.

Television Lesson Utilization

Most sources of information about educational television focus more on *producing* the televised lesson—how the cameras are controlled to pick up the television teacher and the visual or demonstration materials —and less on *utilizing* the televised lesson. But actually, there are far fewer studio teachers who appear on camera than there are classroom teachers who must use incoming televised lessons effectively with their pupils.

The pupils in the classroom see both the television teacher and the classroom teacher, and the two must seem to work together to create the situation best for learning. If the classroom teacher turns the set to the proper channel at the proper time and then, without further word, retreats to the rear of the classroom to catch up on administrative work or grading, the pupils soon sense the relative importance of the televised lesson to the local classroom scene and will respond accordingly with almost the exact reverse of the usual behavior—doing homework while they are supposed to be watching television.

Actually, the task of proper utilization begins long before the lesson is received. Usually, the decision to make televised lessons available is not made by the classroom teacher, but by curriculum specialists in the school system, who either produce or contract for existing series. While the same objective, that of matching televised lessons to the pupils' level of advancement applies to television as it does to other instructional materials, there is with television a somewhat greater leeway. Learning from television, which involves listening skills and attention, is not as dependent upon reading achievement level as is learning from textbooks, wherein there is fairly close grading. A fourth grade televised science lesson might well be useful for grades ranging from two to six if the content corresponds closely enough to the local curriculum. An accelerated class might appropriately use materials of a higher indicated grade than is suitable for a slow class.

While the individual classroom teacher cannot usually determine which instructional television series will be available via one of the various dissemination systems, the power of specific lesson selection remains open, and the classroom teacher should be discriminating in using lessons that contribute to a given learning situation. Most televised series are not structured so that every single lesson must be used. In those cases where each lesson is not contingent upon the information in the preceding one, the classroom teacher should feel free to draw upon the televised lessons as they fit into the following categories of uses:

1. to capture, stimulate, and maintain interest for pupil motivation;
2. to form the core presentation of content in a given unit;
3. to serve as a synthesizing or culminating activity.

Having determined the purpose and context for the classroom use of the televised lessons, the teacher has to pay particular attention to the teaching manuals that are ordinarily provided in connection with a television series. Manuals are of critical importance for televised lessons, for unlike films, filmstrips, phonograph records, and most other instructional media, televised lessons received from a broadcast or cable source cannot be previewed directly by the teacher as a regular part of lesson preparation. A good television manual will give the objectives of the lesson, the special vocabulary used, key questions that pupils usually ask (with suggested answers!), outline of the content, bibliography, the charts and diagrams that are displayed during the televised lessons and which should be available later for reference, additional readings, follow-up activities, and tests. With this material, the teacher is in a good position to determine prospective values of the lesson for particular pupils at a particular time, and to plan what to do in class immediately prior to the televised lesson, during pupil viewing, and immediately afterward.

Prior to the lesson, the classroom teacher needs to perform several tasks:

1. Make technical preparations. Check the performance of the set by turning it to the proper channel at least fifteen minutes prior to the scheduled start of the lesson. Make proper adjustments for sound and picture as on a home set. Then turn the volume control all the way down and turn the brightness knob all the way to blackness. The result will be a blank and silent set, but one that is known to be working and that needs only two quick, minor adjustments to be in full operation. If the set doesn't work properly, finding this out fifteen minutes before the start of the actual lesson will usually allow time either to summon the person in the building who can make the right adjustments or to bring in a spare or presently unused set. If the set cannot be made to work at all and there is no spare, at least the pre-telecast time has not been wasted building the class up for an activity that cannot take place.

2. Get the class ready. Have the pupils put away all of the things that they will not need during the television presentation—objects that will distract some and annoy others. Work out with the class the standards for viewing behavior, pointing out how viewing in school differs from home viewing, where the primary purpose is relaxation and entertainment. If the manual has indicated that pupil responses are required during the lesson, such as singing along with the television teacher during the music lesson, prepare them and possibly practice with them. If the televised lessons contain programmed elements, have the pupils ready to work problems, make choices, and write answers on their worksheets. Do the same for all indicated motor responses.

3. Provide the required prior information. The vocabulary and important new ideas and concepts that may be unfamiliar in the lesson should be introduced beforehand if there is indication that they might raise questions that cannot be answered during the actual televised lesson. This does not mean to pre-teach the lesson, but to foster interest and generate recognition when potentially puzzling items are used in the lesson. An effective pre-telecast session makes the pupils ready and eager for the actual lesson preparation.

While the children are viewing the televised lesson, the classroom teacher does not take time out; rather, he should be an active viewer

Hawaii Department of Education

Utilization

A fifth grade classroom teacher at the Hokulani Elementary School in Hawaii reviews the vocabulary introduced during the telecast of lesson 11, "The Male," of the ETV series "A Time of Your Life," produced by KQED, San Francisco.

also, for the pupils will emulate their model. The teacher can encourage pupils to engage in the desired response activities. And most importantly, the teacher can learn as much as visual observation of overt behavior allows about individual pupil learning problems. With the television teacher assuming the main burden for information presentation during the lesson, the experienced classroom teacher can spend a good share of the time watching for the frown, the shrug, the idle stare into space. These are indicators that individual assistance may subsequently be needed.

The time to follow up a television lesson is at the moment of its conclusion. With the set turned off, the teacher can begin with the questions and other activities planned to clarify, reaffirm, expand, and apply the material of the lesson. The classroom teacher has more critical things to do at this point than to attempt to reteach the lesson in different words, and the temptation to do this should be resisted. Immediate application of the content by working problems and engaging in purposeful discussion will indicate to the teacher whether or not the points of the lesson are understood. Such immediate application reinforces good in-school television viewing behavior, for the pupil knows that he will be called upon to perform and to use what he learns from television.

Local Production and Videotaping

The increasing use of the portable videotape recorder is opening a new dimension in classroom television. Television lessons can now be

Videotape Recording of Pupils in the Classroom

Pupils are highly motivated to share their progress with others by video-taping their activities for playback to the class, and for talking over with their teacher, as shown here taking place at the Arevalos School in Huntington Beach, California.

Especially popular subject areas for pupil videotape recording are drama, music, and physical education, where the "instant replay" techniques of professional sports telecasts allow pupils to check their own strong and weak points.

as accessible as films. A growing number of educational television centers are transmitting lessons by broadcast or closed circuit at off-hours specifically so that local schools can record the lessons on their own videotape recorders for playback as needed. Not only can the lesson so recorded be used at the particular time desired by the classroom teacher, but the lesson can be repeated when additional study, review, and make-up opportunities are indicated. With the addition of a simple camera, pictures can be originated on the spot and recorded for immediate or delayed playback. Demonstrations that are costly or lengthy to perform can be done once and recorded, with each pupil afforded a close-up view of the critical elements. During editing, redundant elements can be deleted.

But perhaps the most appreciable value of the in-class camera and portable videotape recorder is in performance analysis and evaluation, especially in speech, in athletics, in drama, and in dance. The instant replay allows self-confrontation for feedback of evaluative information at the proper time and in the most direct way for acceptance and correction, because the pupil can spot his own weaknesses and take positive steps toward improvement. In addition, classroom television origination and recording allows pupil creative work with media for role playing and creative dramatics, leading to an enhanced self-image and understanding among pupils from diverse social and cultural backgrounds.

From the simple classroom camera to the full-studio production appears to be a great chasm. Yet it can be bridged by creative instructional production techniques. A complete television lesson can be made by the teacher alone, using a production console specially designed for this purpose. Such a console employs an overhead camera with zoom lens to pick up (either directly or through a mirror) a wide variety of visual materials arranged on the top surface. A head-on camera picks up the image of the teacher. Using a simple switcher to send either picture to classrooms or the videotape recorder, the teacher has at his fingertips an origination capability of considerable flexibility, all the while retaining control of the television process.

As is the case with film, television presents the schools with a challenge and an opportunity to develop wise consumers of the media. Programs broadcast over both commercial and public television stations are of considerable usefulness in relation to class assignments, as well as to artistic merit. The television film documentary is a particularly powerful and timely vehicle for instruction. Dramatic and musical specials bring cultural resources into the home in unparalleled quantity and quality. Television guides prepared especially for teachers are available for the key broadcast programs that are of interest to teachers and pupils.

Teacher-Controlled Television Console

This specially designed console permits the teacher to control the elements of a televised lesson.

The head-on remotely controlled camera picks up a picture of the teacher, who by looking into the lens, gives the viewing pupils the impression that he is talking directly to them.

On the console, a camera recessed into back of the top shoots up into an overhead mirror to pick up the reflected image of a portion of the working surface in front of the teacher. A zoom lens enables the pickup area to vary from postage stamp size to a large writing tablet. When the teacher wants to display visual materials, he switches from the head-on camera to the console camera, and the picture on the receiving sets is instantaneously changed.

Locally Produced Videotape Lesson Materials

Classroom laboratory experiments in high school chemistry are picked up by the small television camera (upper left) and recorded directly on the portable television tape recorder (foreground).

In the Okefenokee Science Curriculum Project, Georgia teachers in cooperating schools prepare curriculum materials by taking the television camera and recorder to field locations.

Students in the Johnny Appleseed School and Training Center at Fort Wayne, Indiana, are able to study repeated playbacks of videotaped materials showing correct job skills procedures.

Classroom Self-Evaluation

An elementary teacher in the Albany, New York, area is recorded while teaching her regular class, using equipment supplied by the Capital District Regional Supplementary Educational Center. Students, teacher aides, and student teachers have all served as operators.

Donald E. Hess, Jr.

Later, she and colleagues critique her handling of classroom situations captured on videotape, often seeing things unobservable while teaching. Tapes are also played for parents, enabling them to see their children in school and to understand the teacher's problems.

Donald E. Hess, Jr.

8

Graphics, Displays, and Exhibits

Today there are many different ways of producing and using instructional visuals in the classroom. The modern teacher should find many applications for such visuals as still pictures, pictorial displays, charts, graphs, diagrams, murals, and cartoons. Visuals are valuable for a number of reasons. They easily attract attention and thus tend to concentrate the interest of the viewer. They can be used to illustrate relationships, similarities, and contrasts between various phenomena. They can relate abstract symbols to concrete objects. Visuals can convey messages that would be all but impossible to communicate with words. And visuals can simply and easily convey a message that really packs a wallop as in the case of cartoons and realistic pictures.

Using Still Pictures

Still pictures are a very valuable resource for the teacher. They are readily available in a wide variety of magazines and other publications. They are one media form the teacher does not have to order or produce; he need only tear them out of the publication and bring them to class. It is a good idea for the teacher to maintain a picture file in his classroom, and pupils can contribute to the building of the file. In a way, the use of pictures gives the teacher his most up-to-date medium, for a picture from the morning newspaper can be used to lead into a lesson.

One reason pictures are so useful is that it is easy to learn from them. Children are quite familiar with pictures long before they begin to read. In fact, literacy is not really necessary to learn from pictures. People who do not share a common language can draw similar meanings from pictures. As a consequence, pictures have often been called a "universal language."

When choosing pictures, the teacher can apply several criteria. First, he should choose a picture for a specific purpose so that he can judge whether or not the information it contains is relevant and important to the learning desired. Pictures should be accurate and authentic in the information they contain. They should be relatively simple so that the vital elements will readily be apparent to the viewer. And the content should be interesting enough so as to maintain the interest of the viewer. Finally, pictures should be of good technical quality, attractive, and large enough to be seen by the class. Although the opaque projector permits enlarged projection of small pictures, it is not as desirable as having large pictures for direct viewing.

The rules or principles for using still pictures in teaching are quite similar to those for using other media. An important difference, however, is the fact that still pictures obviously are not transient in the sense that films and television are. Consequently, pupils can have a relatively long period of time to analyze the pictures and they can work at their own speed. When using still pictures, then, the teacher should not supply a running commentary as is characteristic in documentary films. Rather, he should, through the use of specific questions and comments, evoke participation by the pupils in identifying items in the pictures, in contrasting and comparing the similarities and differences of elements of the pictures, and in interpreting or drawing inferences from the visual stimuli presented. Perhaps the best use of pictures is to stimulate learners to exercise their powers of observation and expression. Showing pictures of two men might lead to an interesting discussion as to who they are, where they live, what they do for a living, and what their lives are like. A picture of a countryside scene could lead to creative expression in painting or poetry. A single picture of people in various situations as, for instance, on a battleground, in a courtroom, on a construction site, or at an airport, could provide endless opportunities for teachers to develop capabilities of creativeness in learners.

Because they are so readily available, still pictures are an excellent medium for involving learners, either independently or in small groups, in different types of projects. Pupils can collect pictures on different topics and then make reports to the class. In science, this could be a series that illustrates the sequence of activities and events in a space flight around the moon. In mathematics, pictures could illustrate different types of applications in areas where a knowledge of mathematics is essential. In social studies, a picture story on conditions and problems of the community could be put together. The possibilities are numerous, and the imaginative teacher should have no trouble finding many opportunities to involve his students in such learning experiences.

The popularity and usefulness of still pictures has resulted in the development of picture sets by commercial producers. These sets include large, colorful prints of excellent quality, and are accompanied by teaching suggestions.

Developing Graphic Visuals

There are several skills in the production of instructional visuals that would be very helpful to the teacher. These include the development and construction of charts and graphs, drawings and cartoons, as well as possessing a knowledge of methods to reproduce printed matter. Skill in constructing models, dioramas, exhibits, and the like would also be very helpful. With these skills, the teacher has a great tool to increase interest and to enhance learning in his classroom. One need not be an accomplished artist in order to produce acceptable graphics and visual displays, however. A little learning goes a long way in this area, and there are several fundamentals which most teachers can learn and apply.

The fundamental characteristics of a visual display include balance, unity, harmony, clarity, and simplicity. Balance refers to the positioning of the elements of a visual to form a particular composition. Two types of balance, formal and informal, are used in visuals. Unity is the integration of the elements of a display into a comprehensive whole. Harmony implies the use of elements which blend together well and which do not appear incongruous for any reason. Clarity is important to ensure easy interpretation. Visuals that are complex or confusing may inhibit learning by causing misunderstandings, or they may fail to teach simply because they are innately less interesting. Normally, visual displays should be limited to one important topic or concept. Simplicity is important for clarity of communication and it can be controlled by limiting the number of visuals used in a display and also by limiting the number of elements included in a single visual.

There are several physical characteristics of a graphic visual that teachers should consider and utilize when creating a visual. The first of these is space. Anyone designing an instructional visual obviously works on a certain amount of space while locating or arranging the elements. These visual elements should not be so large or so numerous as to fill up the available space. A fair amount of blank space should be left around the border to give the visual the appearance of unity and to avoid creating a crowded look. Also, elements of a visual receive added emphasis and importance when they are surrounded by relatively large areas of blank space.

One of the simplest and yet most powerful tools for the teacher who is creating visuals is the use of lines. Simple line drawings can be very effective communicators, and virtually everyone can develop some skill in creating them. Lines are used to form shapes, to suggest action, to focus attention and control eye movement, and to add visual strength or structure. Variations in the direction, thickness, and color of a line are sufficient to suggest different moods.

Another important characteristic of a visual element is shape because it supplies the means by which the element is recognized. Frequently, the outline of an object is the most significant communications feature about it. Visuals do not necessarily need to be realistic to be good communicators, and so a designer can add interest and emphasis by freely interpreting the shapes of objects.

Size is another characteristic that must be considered in designing visuals. Size serves as a tool to attract attention and to emphasize the relative importance of the elements of a visual. Very small and very large elements tend to attract a great deal of attention. The most important element in a visual display should normally be made the largest element.

Color is a valuable tool which the teacher can use for a variety of purposes in designing visuals. Color attracts attention, particularly among children. Color can aid visibility by providing contrasts, and it can also be used to show separations and relationships. Color transmits knowledge about different elements because of strong associations that exist in the minds of viewers.

An essential part of creating good visuals is the effective use of lettering for captions, labels, or titles. Again, the teacher need not be highly skilled in order to make use of several lettering tools. These include lettering pens, stencils, mechanical lettering sets, dry transfer letters, and precut letters. When lettering for displays, the teacher should strive for simplicity, clarity, and legibility. Ornate or fancy styles of letters should normally be avoided.

By applying a knowledge of the basic principles and characteristics of visuals discussed above, the average teacher can do much for himself in the production of effective instructional graphics. The various types of graphics include charts, graphs, diagrams, posters, murals, cartoons, and comics. In this chapter, only a few of these will be considered to illustrate their value in teaching.

Graphs

Graphs are used to show visually, numerical or quantitative data and relationships. The most common types include the line graph, the bar graph, the circle graph, and the pictorial graph.

Illustrations of Graphs

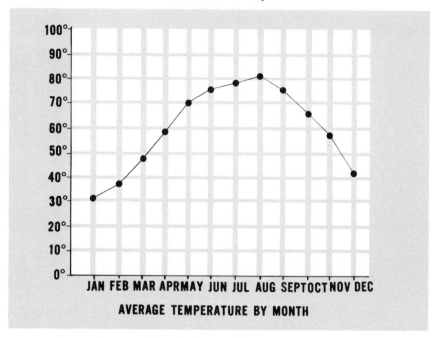

Simple line graph. Dots on the X-Y matrix determine the line.

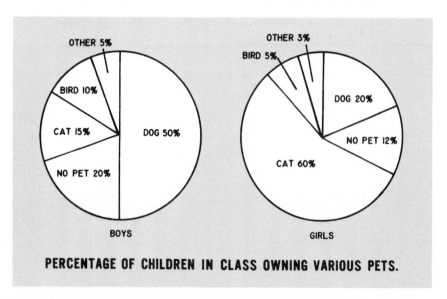

Formal balance in comparison of two circle graphs.

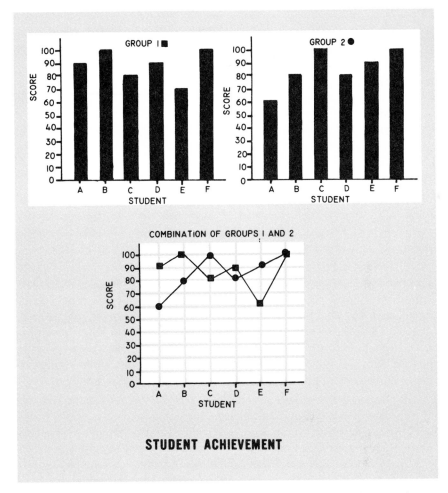

Informal balance in comparison of two bar graphs and one line graph.

Line graphs are particularly valuable for the precise recording of data representing a relationship between two phenomena. Plotting the rise in the cost of living over a period of time, the growth of farm production over a period of time, the relationship of cost to effectiveness in various courses of action, and plotting the curve of a physical formula are some of the common uses of line graphs.

Bar graphs are very simple to produce and to read. They are most useful in comparing quantities or percentages of similar items. Bars of varying lengths, but of the same width, are drawn from a base line, and the length of the bars serves to illustrate the quantitative relationships. Bar graphs should normally be used to compare not more than about seven or eight items in order to keep the graph readable.

A circle graph is simply a circle cut into two or more sectors wherein the size of the sectors represents percentage or fractional portions of some whole. The entire circle obviously must always represent 100 percent of some entity. Circle graphs are very useful for purposes such as depicting the percentage of the world's automobiles found in the different countries and continents, or for showing the proportion of the country's population in various age groups.

Pictorial graphs employ picture-like symbols to represent quantities. Simple outline figures of men, women, ships, planes, animals, food products, or any other object can be used to represent an arbitrary number of items. Such pictorial illustrations are useful for depicting increases or declines in population or production of goods and for comparing such quantities between countries, or over a span of time.

In either choosing or constructing a graph for teaching purposes, simplicity and clarity are two of the most important considerations. Graphs that are excessively complex or that contain too much trivial detail will be much more difficult to read and interpret. When constructing graphs, a teacher must take particular care to use a scale that is consistent with the types of data to be related; otherwise a distorted picture can occur. A common mistake, or distortion, is the failure to begin at zero in plotting a set of data on a line or bar graph.

By its nature, a graph summarizes large amounts of data. It is not a very colorful or exciting media form, and so a teacher would not normally use a graph to stimulate or motivate at the beginning of a lesson. After pupils have acquired a general knowledge of the subject, graphs can be used to nail down some of the concrete quantitative aspects. The use of other media, such as films and pictures, is recommended for the earlier stages of learning.

Charts and Diagrams

There are several different types of charts that are useful in teaching. These include organization charts, flow charts, tabular charts, and chronology charts. Organization charts, as the name implies, are used mainly to illustrate the structure of organizations. A flow chart is used to depict the sequence of events in some process such as, for example, manufacturing a product, programming a computer, or designing an instructional sequence. Tabular charts are used to compare or relate lists of items which have a sequential, functional, or other type of relationship. A tabular chart could be used, for example, to show the various subject matter topics that comprise the curriculum for the first twelve years of schooling. A chronology or time chart relates events to a span of time. It can be used to show the development of a science or technology, to relate important inventions in a time sequence, and for similar uses.

One particular type of chart construction that is worth mentioning is the flip chart which enables the teacher to expose the various items or steps in a lesson one at a time according to his own scheduling. This technique is valuable in a situation where a considerable amount of information must be presented or where there is a sequence of pupil activity to accompany the charts. Unlike standard charts, which may be self-instructional or which may serve as a visual accompaniment to the lecture, flip charts are used primarily as an adjunct to the instructor's oral presentation.

A diagram is a simplified drawing, usually involving lines and symbols, which depicts functional or spacial relationships. A circuit diagram is a common example, as is an engineering blueprint. A football coach diagrams plays on a chalkboard, using X's and 0's with lines added. Because diagrams rely on symbols for communication, it is essential that pupils have adequate background in the subject matter including, obviously, a knowledge of the symbols employed. It is also a good idea to use pictorial media, such as a slide series, along with diagrams to show realistic pictures of the elements symbolized in the diagrams.

Visual Displays

The visual display is a combination of visual elements, including pictures, graphs, diagrams, print, graphic symbols, and three-dimensional objects, displayed in permanent form (for the life of the display) in the classroom. Such displays serve several purposes. First of all, they dress up a room and serve as dramatic indicators that teachers and pupils are involved in interesting and meaningful activities. Displays can serve as thematic organizers to guide study through a particular unit. The different concepts depicted can provide areas for research on the part of individuals or small groups. Displays of good size, color, and composition can give emphasis to concepts, ideas, or topics that are normally given little or no attention by pupils. The nature of life in a country that is just a speck on the map can be vividly portrayed by a good display. In this way, pupil interest and motivation can be enhanced.

When developing visual displays, the teacher ought to consider a number of important points. First, he must identify the specific idea or concept to be communicated. A visual display should be simple and

Pupil-Made Displays

As a first step in making an illustrated wall display, pupils trace the image of an outline map of New England projected from an overhead transparency.

Bell and Howell

A colored fabric-covered panel on an adjustable aluminum easel forms the background for a creative social studies display. A small swatch of adhesive backed Hook tape permits letters and three-dimensional objects to be affixed easily to the panel.

Charles Mayer Studios, Inc.

PRODUCTS MADE IN OUR CITY

should generally concentrate on one central theme. The more specific the teacher can be in identifying this idea, the better position he will be in to develop a successful display. For example, an objective such as "to depict the advance of technology in the twentieth century" may be a commendable one but one which is just too broad to give much direction as to how one is to depict it and how one is to gauge that the pupils have understood the message. An objective such as "to document the various phases of an Apollo moon flight" is much more specific and thus more suitable. It is a good idea for the teacher to ask himself if the effects of the display can readily be described in terms of potential learner competence. Since it is easy to test whether or not a pupil can state or describe the phases of an Apollo flight, it is easy to tell if the display is effective in the communication for which it was intended. Of course, many displays may not be intended to serve as total learning experiences. They may merely serve to identify areas for further study and research, in which case the teacher would not attempt to isolate and measure the effect of the display alone.

It is important that the teacher, when developing a display, consider the pupils' interests and backgrounds. Whenever possible, pupils should be involved in the planning of the display and in gathering materials for it. They are sure to select items that interest them. Since more than enough materials will likely be brought in, the class can have a valuable experience in deciding what materials to use, why to use them, and how to use them.

As with all graphic materials, a cardinal rule for making an effective display is to keep it simple. The temptation to overload the display with good copy just because it is available must be resisted. The material that is included should make an impact on pupils, should impel them to stop and view it for a period of time, and should motivate them to want to do further study. The material must contain enough information to get the class involved in studying it; it is not enough that it be merely attractive. It should cause the pupils to think and develop further questions, questions that can be answered through research in a library, museum, or other source.

The size and location of a display are, of course, important physical considerations. The size should be adequate so as to contain a substantial amount of information without having the display become cluttered or crowded, and to attract attention at a moderate distance. The display must be located where it will readily be seen and where it is possible for the class to view it for several minutes or whatever time is essential to accomplish the teaching purpose.

The same characteristics of good design that were discussed in the previous section relative to balance, unity, use of color and space, should

Houghton Mifflin Company

Manipulative Models

Houghton Mifflin Company

Mathematical concepts are often more readily comprehended when pupils manipulate three-dimensional representations. Packaged sets of models aid both demonstration and discovery.

An accurate, detailed full-color model of the torso of a 12-year-old boy is ideal for teaching biology, health, physiology, and first aid.

Functional components of the eye are enlarged and keyed in this classroom model which has removable parts to demonstrate vision.

Hubbard Scientific Company

Hubbard Scientific Company

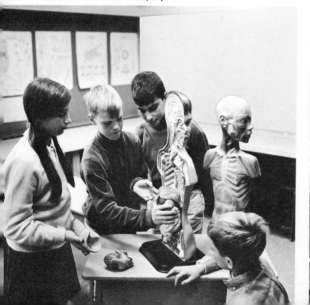

The ultimate instructional models and environmental exhibits are found in musseums, which are favorite spots for curriculum-supporting field trips.

Visiting pupils watch the operation of the Cube of Lights model in the IBM mathematics exhibit at the Museum of Science and Industry, Chicago. By pushing a combination of buttons on a control panel, they can visually experience the number being added, multiplied, or squared in the 512 blinking lights of the model.

Museum of Science and Industry, Chicago

Museum of Science and Industry, Chicago

Young visitors examine a 16-foot-tall model of the human heart, which forms part of the medical display. They not only learn how the heart functions, but by amplified recordings, can also hear it throb.

be considered in multielement visual displays. Furthermore, such displays should contain appropriate captions in the form of provocative questions or statements, to attract attention, to identify the theme of the display, and to suggest the theme or purpose of further work on the topic.

There are several different ways in which visual presentations may be displayed in the classroom. The familiar bulletin board technique involves pinning or pasting materials to a smooth surface. The chalkboard can be used for displays and sketches in addition to its more common usage as a place to present information or to have children work problems. The flannel board is a convenient display tool which allows the teacher to add items as he develops a presentation; however, it is somewhat limited by the fact that it depends on the adhesion of two pieces of flannel or felt. An improvement of this concept is represented by the hook and loop board which provides numerous small loops into which display elements can be hooked for support. What the individual teacher decides to use will depend on his own teaching style and on what is available in his school building.

Environmental Exhibits

Displays move into another dimension when they include multimedia forms of information presentation and when they increase in size so as to envelop the viewer or to program his movements through an exhibit. Environmental exhibits of this type are most common in world's fairs and in industrial exhibitions; and quite frequently, exhibit vans from health or public safety bureaus visit schools.

In some museums, there are large scale models of various objects or localities, and these are often combined with motion pictures, slides, and sound. The models themselves may be cut-away forms with operating parts and are usually of gigantic scale. There is one model of the human heart, for example, that is so large that a pupil can learn about the workings of that organ by walking through huge replicas of the chambers and arteries. On the other hand, the process of coal mining can be studied by persons visiting a museum's full-scale operating construction of a coal mine.

When such environmental exhibits are in museums and exhibition halls, the teacher may conduct a field trip to ensure that all pupils have that experience. However, such learning experiences are highly motivational for children and their parents as out-of-school activities. The point here is that, unlike a field trip that takes a class to an actual activity, this kind of field trip takes the pupil to a mediated one which is especially designed to increase his interest and to enhance his learning.

9

Instructional
Systems and Multimedia

Throughout this book, an emphasis has been placed on the need for incorporating media into a systematic plan for achieving educational outcomes, for treating a media instrument as an element of a total learning system. A complete instructional system includes a listing of objectives, an instructional program designed to achieve these objectives, all media and materials relevant to the program, provision for teacher-learner interaction, and an evaluation plan with suitable test items. All of these components should be compatible and should be validated in terms of their contribution to the total system. The most rigorous attempt to develop such validated instructional systems has been the programmed instruction movement.

Programmed Instruction and Teaching Machines

Programmed instruction has been described as a system, as a concept, and as a process. The important point is that it should not be considered as being another type of media. The concept can be applied in any media form. Programs have commonly been characterized as *linear*, usually consisting of small steps, each with a blank to be filled in, or as *branching*, presenting page-length frames each of which is followed by a multiple-choice question. While programs frequently take one of these forms, this description does not explain the underlying principles of program development.

Probably the two most important concepts inherent in programmed instruction are *quality control* and *empirical validation*. Before a program is written, objectives are prepared in terms of pupil behavior, and the program is tested and revised until it can be shown that satisfactory results are obtained each time the program is used with a proper learner population. Then the program is said to be validated. Quality control of the program is maintained by measuring the effect of each stimulus-response element. Therefore, the idea of using small steps makes it easier to pinpoint the parts of the program that are working and those that are not and that need to be revised. Once a program is completed and validated, it can be assumed with relative safety that it will always be effective in achieving a particular set of objectives with a particular set of learners. Consequently, when purchasing programs for school use, educators should insist on a list of objectives that the program is intended to achieve *and also* on data that indicate the degree of success achieved with the learners involved in the validation process.

Programmed instruction may be entirely in paper form, such as a programmed textbook, or it may require a teaching machine to present it. The teaching machine is not a medium in itself. It may involve the use of paper and print as a means of presenting stimuli and eliciting responses, or it may have a projection screen and employ film in some form or other. Pupil response may be made on paper with a pencil, or by pressing a button, or even by touching a point on a cathode ray display tube. The teaching machine, however, merely acts as a costly mechanical page-turner unless it records pupil responses and selects the next frame from a substantial bank of examples or instructional se-‘ quences based on the individual pupil's pattern of responses.

This type of capability calls not only for a complex display utilizing cathode ray display tubes or rapid print-out units, but also highly sophisticated information processing which only a computer can provide. Computer-assisted instruction is not different from programmed instruction—let alone a different *medium*—but instead it represents an advanced approach to the presentation of programmed materials and the processing of pupil responses. The main contributions of the computer are those of facilitating pupil access through remote terminals, keeping track of pupil progress, assessing initial pupil abilities and developing them, providing with infinite patience rapid branching of instructional sequences and teaching examples based on analysis of patterns of pupil responses, and recording data for evaluation of the program as well as of the pupil.

In discussing teaching machines and computer-assisted instruction, a distinction has been made between *hardware* (the equipment) and *software* (the operating procedures and instructional materials). The hardware, with its blinking lights, glowing tubes, and shiny knobs and buttons, creates its own fascination. But the computer itself does not teach; the materials are the key to pupil learning. Like all programmed materials, but even more so, the software of computer-assisted instruction is costly in energy, time, and money. Whereas it may have taken forty hours or more of programming time to produce one hour of pupil

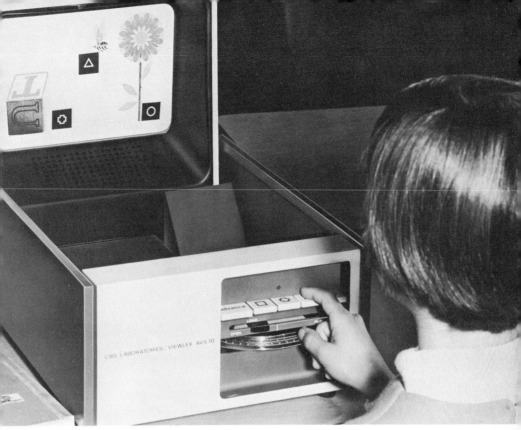

CBS Laboratories/Viewlex

While the first teaching machines did little more than control the presentation of a printed program, newer versions provide sound and pictures, with mechanisms for students to indicate active responses.

Responsive Environments Corporation

The "Talking Page" is a multisensory responsive learning system that provides the learner with self-pacing, audiovisual programmed instruction.

participation time to use paper and pencil programs or audiovisual instruments such as an audiotape coordinated with a programmed workbook, it now takes approximately four hundred hours of development time to produce computer-assisted materials for one pupil hour at the console. This thorough planning-programming-tryout-revise process yields software for computer-assisted instruction that is typically much more effective than conventional materials.

Few teachers have had the opportunity to come in contact with computers or other sophisticated machines in education. Most teachers who use programmed instruction do so in the form of programmed textbooks or workbooks. There are several ways that such a program could be used in instruction. It could constitute the entire content of a particular course or it could be a unit or module within a course. A program could be used as enrichment for more advanced pupils or as a remedial device for pupils lacking in prerequisites for a particular course.

There are several things to keep in mind when using programs in the classroom. Not all pupils will display equal ease and facility in learning from programs, and so other types of activities should also be planned. Because programs have built-in participation, the teacher should make plans to utilize effectively the time that programs release in assisting learners on an individual or small group basis. If a pupil has difficulty with a program, he is likely to be more frustrated than he would be, for example, viewing a film that contains some concepts he does not understand. Therefore, a teacher should be sure that a program fits the abilities of his pupils, and he must keep a close watch on their progress to detect any difficulties. Also, it should be made clear that a program is a learning instrument, not a test. Responses made in programs should never be graded. They are intended to provide practice of behaviors that will be tested later.

Multimedia Approaches to Instruction

The term, multimedia, means a combination of various types of media arranged so as to provide appropriate presentational capability to realize the objectives and content of a lesson through eliciting desired pupil responses. The key factor in a properly designed multimedia arrangement is not simply the use of more than one kind of audiovisual device. It is the interrelationship of the media used in order to capitalize on the distinctive characteristics and capabilities of each, making them mutually supportive in the creation of a new learning environment.

The simplest form of multimedia use is the combining of two audiovisual devices in order to take advantage of the presentational capabilities of each. An example is the sound filmstrip, which combines the sound from a phonodisc or audiotape with the automatic or manually advanced filmstrip, as described in Chapter 4. The audio device—phonograph or tape recorder—provides a relatively inexpensive way to add sound to the series of projected pictures. A single device, the sound motion picture projector, can provide this capability, plus motion, but at approximately ten times higher cost of materials for individual presentations. But theoretically and practically, it is a waste of money and media capability to use the motion picture medium for this purpose unless actual motion in the presentation is relevant and necessary.

Upon analysis, many times such motion is not necessary to learning if the critical points to learn in a process are a series of discrete steps. For instance, a presentation to instruct pupils on the correct procedure for wiring an electrical circuit can well be handled by the sound filmstrip, for the action required by the learners is a series of specific things to do. The very clarity and definition of still pictures can contribute to rapid mastery of each step as one after another forms the complete process. On the other hand, a presentation of the proper techniques for typing, sewing, or operating a lathe requires actual motion, because the desired action is more than a series of steps and involves continuous movement. Having the capability to arrange multimedia effectively allows the teacher and media specialists to make decisions on this basis.

Another utilization of the multimedia concept does not result from the physical combination of media but rather from the careful sequencing of a variety of media which forms an integrated package or kit of materials correlated to achieve a specific set of objectives. For example, in a geography lesson on land forms, the teacher might move from a world globe to a regional map, then show a motion picture, and follow this with still pictures and even a 3-D model, all of which are carefully correlated to textbook readings. In this way, the teacher in the school without elaborate hardware systems can still take advantage of the different presentational capabilities of different media to provide the stimulus-response elements essential to learning.

The most dramatic use of multimedia is in the combination of projection media to present multiple simultaneous images. Using a series of smaller screens on a single large wall projection area, a battery of slides, motion pictures, and even television projectors can bombard the viewers with images, and by filling all areas of peripheral vision, seem to engulf them in the visual experience. Because of the ease with which multimedia projection, coupled with mixed stereo sound, can produce such dramatic effects, it is important when using multimedia for instructional use to keep clearly in mind the purpose of the particular presentation and to measure the contribution of each element toward that purpose. It is also helpful to devise a plan for the use of multiple images in instruction, based on the following suggestions as to how two or more screens can be used:

1. To hold an overview shot or complete picture on one screen, such as a laboratory experiment arrangement, while moving to a series of detailed close-up pictures on the other.
2. To show two pictures side by side for comparison, such as two works of art, each on a separate slide.
3. To hold a title of a group classification on one screen, with a series of example pictures on the other screen, providing a sort of visual paragraphing.
4. To show a line-drawing or labeled schematic diagram of an object or organism next to an actual photograph.
5. To show three to six different photographs to convey a range of examples; any or all can be changed as desired.
6. To display a picture while showing a series of questions or factual notes on a second screen.

The teacher should be in command of the multimedia presentation. The exotic projection onto the multiple screens or large projection surface should not diminish the use of the overhead projector for direct teacher control of transparency display, manipulation, and information addition. Control of multimedia projectors can be done remotely by manual switches and buttons on the teacher's lectern, or automatically by pre-punched programmed cards on a master control device. The projectors may be located in a projection booth in the rear of the room (or on a specially designed platform or cart arrangement if there is no booth) for front-throw projection. But an increasingly popular method is to use a large translucent screen across the front of the room with the bank of projectors located behind it for rear-screen projection. Rear-screen projection requires special design consideration for light paths, throw distances, light control, and equipment arrangement, including mirrors for motion picture projection (an image projected directly onto a rear screen will appear reversed from the audience point of view on the other side of the screen). Rear-screen projection allows a higher degree of ambient light in the room, a circumstance which is especially helpful if pupils have to take notes.

Pupil Response Systems

A highly significant capability of multimedia is the regularizing and quantifying of information on individual learning. Pupil response

Student Response Systems

Advanced classroom communication systems complete the instructional loop to provide information about student learning. By means of five-button student responder units located at each seat, the student selects a coded response, and the resulting data is displayed for immediate feedback to the teacher and recorded for record keeping and evaluation purposes. The programmer tape unit can control various synchronized audiovisual projectors.

Dr. Charles Stamps

Multimedia Support for Large Group Sessions

Behind the large rear-screen area in the front of the main auditorium of Northeastern Illinois State College is a battery of slide, motion picture, and television projectors programmed for multiple-image display as controlled from the instructor's lectern.

systems allow the teacher to question the class and determine at once, not only *how many* pupils are able to arrive at the correct response, but *which specific* pupils, and data records are kept accordingly.

Pupil response systems enable the teacher to pose a question, for example, and obtain feedback from pupils who turn an indicator or depress a button to select one of several alternate responses. The questions can call for a multiple-choice answer, or they can ask for a reaction by asking "Do you understand?" or "Have you finished working the problem?" The responses are recorded in digital or analogue form and can be read out by the teacher or computed in data processing machines so as to maintain a record of pupil work.

School Learning Resource Centers

As a place for facilitating individualized instruction, the traditional school library is expanding into a learning resources center, with media systems complementing standard book materials and periodicals. A popular feature of the learning resources center is the individual pupil multimedia carrel. Recent advances in design make it possible for a rear screen located at the back surface of the carrel to display images projected from slide, cartridge film, and filmstrip projectors, in combination with cassette audiotape recorders. Materials forming a multimedia package are checked out from a central desk. The packages may contain loaded slide trays, audiotape cartridges, filmstrips, film loops, and so forth, together with instructional notebooks. When the same lesson is to be used by large numbers of pupils, some carrels may be reserved exclusively for a particular course or unit and so will always be set up and ready for such use.

The learning resources center may be the location of remote terminals for computer-assisted instruction described previously. Advanced information systems make use of the carrels for remote access to electronically distributed instructional materials. In such carrels, the materials are not taken physically to the carrel, but instead are accessed by dialing a preassigned number on a control panel in the carrel, and the lesson material appears on a television screen and/or is heard via headphones. In dial-access systems, audio and video materials are stored on tape in a central information center and are individually activated.

A distinction may be made between *dial access* and *random access* of instructional materials in individualized learning systems. The dial, or touch-tone panel, may enable the individual pupil in the carrel to tune in a particular program. If he is the first to do so, his signal activates the tape machine, and the lesson starts; but another pupil dialing the same number minutes later hears or sees the program already in

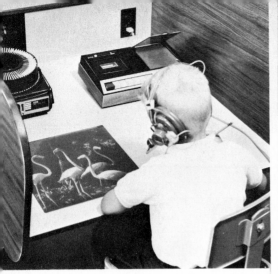

owledge Aid Division of Radiant Corporation   Knowledge Aid Division of Radiant Corporation

Learning Carrels for Individualized Study

In a self-contained multimedia learning carrel, both the materials and equipment are physically located in the carrel for direct operation by the pupil. Here a fourth-grader works through an art lesson using an audio cassette to present instructions and to drive the synchronized slide projector, which projects into a series of mirrors to display the images on the working surface of the carrel.

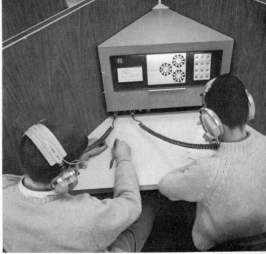

mpex Corporation   Ampex Corporation

In the learning center of Oak Park-River Forest High School in Illinois, a sophisticated audio and video system permits remote random access to stored instructional tapes.

Management of the learning center is facilitated by monitoring, switching, communications, and record-keeping instrumentation.

Link Educational Systems Division, The Singer Company

Simulation

High School driving education pupils learn psychomotor skills involved in automobile handling by means of the driving simulator. Seated in a full-sized section of a driver's control compartment, they respond to motion picture projection of actual traffic situations.

This strange black box is a game-type scientific tool. By probing the pro-grammed environment of the Inquiry Box, which contains few variables and provides a limited number of ways to collect data, pupils from kindergarten through high school can analyze and understand the techniques and pro-cesses of inquiry.

Science Research Associates, Inc.

progress. True random access means that the pupil is always able to tune in the *start* of a program, and individual control means that he is able to stop and restart it at any point, or repeat sections as desired. More sophisticated information systems, with rapid automatic duplication features, permit this capability for audio materials at greatly increased cost, and for video at virtually prohibitive cost. The operational question is this: is it worth the added cost to enable each pupil to dial in at the start of the lesson *at the time of his own choosing,* or is it acceptable to make programs available on a frequently scheduled basis—every half hour, for example, and thus require only one program source per lesson, rather than one per lesson per pupil station—a geometric increase in equipment requirements?

Simulation

Through simulation, the pupil learning environment in school is made as close as possible to performance conditions outside of school in a real life situation. Simulation is used not only because it saves time and money through conservation of actual field equipment, but also because pupil learning can be carefully controlled and protected from dangers inherent in some particular operations. The driver education simulator teaches the basic operation of the automobile, and through multimedia presentations, guides the pupil toward correct responses. But if he makes mistakes in the simulator when confronting certain road situations, he does not actually crash into a utility pole or run down a pedestrian. One point to remember is that the simulation must lead to actual operation as a part of the structured learning experience if real proficiency is the objective of instruction. Assumptions cannot be made as to the assurance of transfer from simulation to reality.

A new and exciting aspect of the use of simulation in education is the concept of educational games. These games involve school children in role-playing activities which simulate work conditions in industry, government, foreign countries, and the like. Pupils are assigned roles in terms of an occupational specialty—politician, engineer, city planner —or a social role—consumer, civil rights worker—and then they must take action to solve a problem, perform a task, or perhaps defend a point of view. Games that relate to community problems, manufacturing operations, family life, urban planning, economic planning, and other types of activities have been developed.

The concept of educational games provides the teacher with an exciting tool to involve pupils in practical, life-like situations. These games can either be purchased from commercial sources or they can be devised by imaginative teachers and pupils.

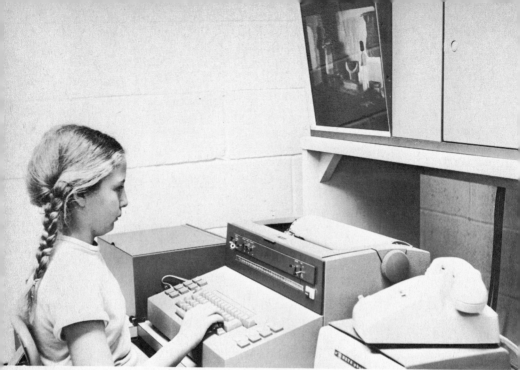

BOCES

Computer-Assisted Game Simulation

A fifth grader types out a response to a question asked her by a computer in the Sumerian social studies game. When she is finished, she will press the top button to her far right. This will send her answer electronically to the computer, which will then respond to her. Scenes like this are occurring at the Board of Cooperative Educational Services, Yorktown Heights, New York.

Computer-Assisted Instruction in Reading

Children who learn reading with the "Talking Typewriter," an advanced computer-assisted learning system, do so voluntarily. In the child's early sessions, he is encouraged to experiment and become familiar with the keyboard. Then the programming system begins to encourage typing of specific letters, and later, words.

Responsive Environments Corporation

10

The Teacher and Media Services

In order to use media effectively in class, the teacher needs several types of services from the media specialists in his school or school system center. Basically, the teacher wants to be able to find out what materials are available; to receive information on the content, value, or quality of the materials; to receive consultation on approaches to selecting and using media in achieving educational goals; to rely on other persons to order materials he has requested and to inform him of their arrival; to depend upon media services to provide technical support in using the materials and related equipment; and to have simple materials produced to his specifications by local production specialists.

In arranging for the services to meet these needs, the teacher will encounter one of three situations: (1) the materials are already available in the school; (2) the materials are available outside the school and must be ordered through purchase, rental, or loan; (3) the materials are not available and so must be custom-produced.

Instructional Media Specialists

A well-organized school system provides the personnel, facilities, and equipment to take care of each of these alternatives. The key figures in the program are the media specialists who operate at both the building and school system levels. As currently defined, a media specialist is a teacher who has broad special professional training in instructional media and whose full-time service is devoted to working in this field. Under the concepts of the Education Professions Development Act of the Federal Government, and supported by standards worked out jointly by the Department of Audiovisual Instruction and the American School Library Association, the school librarian and the audiovisual positions have merged at the professional level to provide the most comprehensive service involving both print and non-print materials. There remain technical specialists for distinctive library or audiovisual tasks, but the overall program represents a unified approach to media support for the teacher.

In large school systems with strong media programs, emphasis is placed on providing direct support to teachers at the building level by establishing an instructional materials center operated by professional media specialists. The teacher should tune in the media specialist to the types of materials that are needed for particular classes, because once alerted, the specialist can serve as an extra pair of eyes searching for appropriate media items. His advice is usually excellent because he is professionally trained for these tasks and devotes full-time effort to them.

In the well-organized instructional materials center are the following: basic textbooks used in the various subjects taught; supplementary reading materials; reference books and encyclopedias; newspapers and periodicals; maps and globes; photographic slides; sound and silent film strips; still pictures; audiotapes and disc recordings; overhead transparencies; motion pictures films, especially 8mm silent loops; charts and posters that have repeated uses; and possibly models and exhibits.

Media specialists also provide services to go with these materials: cataloging, filing, maintaining, and loaning for use the materials owned by the school; ordering and distributing materials from outside sources, such as the school system media centers or university film libraries; giving assistance in locating materials needed for specific teaching situations; providing advice on techniques and criteria for evaluating and selecting materials; and offering consultation on the use of media materials to achieve educational goals.

A teacher should become familiar with the variety of materials and services available in his school's instructional materials center. Frequently, teachers are heard to remark to the instructional resources staff, "We didn't know you had all this right here." The alert teacher does not long remain ignorant of the help that is already at hand.

Supporting the school media specialists are the system media center personnel who not only maintain centralized materials resources, such as the film library, but provide in-service workshops and teachers' meetings, and distribute catalogs and publications. In a system where there are good building level instructional materials centers, there is likely to be a good centrally located office as well.

The teacher needs to work with media specialists, as well as with all other professional specialists in education. This does not mean to assume that the specialists are solely responsible for all of the work in the field. For example, the teacher has to make his needs known with regard to the instructional materials budget. This is not an area where

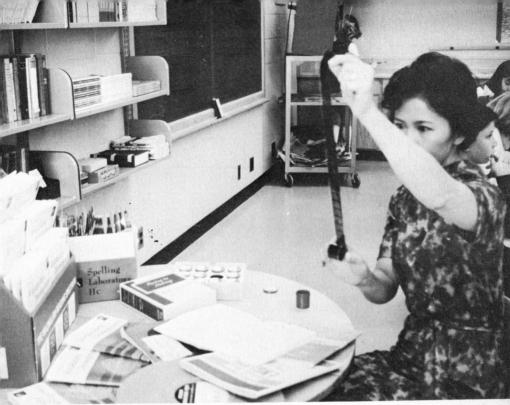

EDUCATION AGE magazine, Visual Products Division, 3M Company.

A Duluth teacher examines a filmstrip in the school learning resources center as part of preparation for writing a "language arts contract" for her pupils.

UICC

In a college demonstration facility, an education student, prior to practice teaching, engages in a self-instructional program to learn how to operate audio-visual equipment.

the teacher should be bashful; when the money's gone, it's too late—at least until next year.

The teacher is well-advised to be on the lookout for media materials through investigations on his own. Most film production companies and distributors are happy to send copies of their catalogs to teachers who request them. The same is true for most publishing companies, commercial organizations, and professional associations that produce useful materials for the classroom—many of which are sponsored so that the catalogs are available free of charge. Of particular value to educators interested in media is the Department of Audiovisual Instruction of the National Education Association in Washington, D. C. Its monthly periodical, *Audiovisual Instruction,* is a useful source of information on new materials, equipment, and utilization techniques. Such agencies as travel offices and embassies can be excellent sources of information and materials on foreign countries.

Obviously, the teacher today is not faced with a problem of shortage of materials in most subject fields. The problem, rather, is to select the best materials and to use them most effectively in the classroom. Media specialists of various types can lend valuable assistance in these areas.

Instructional Materials Production

Through the local production of materials, either by himself or with the assistance of media production specialists, the teacher has a means of quickly obtaining materials that can enhance teaching and learning in his classroom. By producing his own materials, or having them produced, the teacher can get exactly what he wants and can, of course, store the materials for repeated use.

Most of the types of materials that teachers might produce locally have already been discussed in the individual chapters of this book. Some of these will be treated again in this summary to illustrate the wide scope of materials the teacher can consider producing. There are several questions the teacher should ask himself before deciding to produce materials in any appreciable quantity. First, are they useful? Do they add something to the instructional process, something that is not available in existing materials? Secondly, are they feasible to produce, neither too difficult, too expensive, nor too time-consuming? Does it look as though the materials will yield a fair educational return in relation to their cost? If the answer is "yes" to all these questions, then the materials should be produced.

To counterbalance the cost and work of local production, there are several advantages. One is that the materials can be tailor-made to fit a particular educational need or situation. The content and the level of difficulty or sophistication can be geared to a particular group of pupils. Their special interests or their disadvantages can be taken into account in the production of materials for them. Another advantage of local production is that obviously the materials can be made current whereas materials that must be purchased or rented may be outdated. A series of slides taken by a teacher or a school photographer, a series that is current, will probably produce better educational effects than will a motion picture which, while it may be only ten years old, was made with film techniques that are now considered primitive, and whose content is considered ancient history by pupils of today. Young learners have strong reactions of amusement to such seemingly trivial details as outdated clothing styles, and once the instructional rapport has been broken by such a reaction, a media presentation may lose whatever effectiveness it might have had. Also, because content in many areas of learning is expanding and changing at a very rapid rate, teacher-made materials can be as current as the morning newspaper.

Another advantage of local production is that the teacher can decide how materials can be produced in a form that is most appropriate for the teaching that is to take place. Many times, a teacher will use a film, not because a film is the best teaching medium for the situation, but because it happened to be a film that covered the content he wanted to communicate. Or a teacher may find some excellent pictures in a magazine to illustrate some lesson, but the pictures may be so small as to be useless at a distance of more than three feet. With local production capabilities, such pictures can be made into slides enlarged to a size appropriate to being held up in front of the class, or included in a study display, or even included in a television videotape where they are magnified by television camera lenses.

It follows that the teacher who has skill in producing materials or in taking advantage of the production capabilities afforded by his school or system media center has acquired a valuable asset in improving the quality of his instruction.

Audiovisual Equipment Services

The classroom teacher does not have to be a mechanical or electronic genius in order to use modern media equipment effectively. For one thing, newer models of equipment are designed with the school situation in mind and are ruggedly reliable and increasingly simple to use. Any apparent complication is more in the mind of the operator than in the gear itself. No piece of the common types of classroom audiovisual equipment requires the complex behavioral coordination

UICC

The professional media specialist helps the classroom teacher to become aware of available instructional materials described in the catalogs of rental sources and commercial distributors.

Both preventative and repair maintenance by fully-trained audiovisual technicians in the school district media center insure the reliability of equipment operation classroom teachers expect.

UICC

that is demanded for driving a car or operating a zig-zag sewing machine. Anyone who can manage to drive to school in the morning will find no real challenge in learning to operate the audiovisual equipment found there. Then, too, many schools employ student operators or paraprofessionals to assist the teacher in classroom tasks, which include setting up and operating projectors, recorders, and the like. Such services are provided so that the teacher can make more efficient use of his time, not to perform tasks that are beyond the teacher's capabilities.

But the teacher might still feel a certain apprehension about using audiovisual equipment in front of the class. Things mechanical, like things human, can go wrong, and the teacher all too easily visualizes the awkward moments when the class looks on while he and the student operator try to figure out what to do to make things work. With the reliability that is built into modern equipment for classroom use, equipment that is checked out as being in working order before class time will seldom fail during actual classroom operation. Therefore, time spent on checking the operation of the equipment before the class assembles, and then leaving the equipment in a ready position, is time well spent. Projection lamps will burn out according to their life expectancy and should not be considered equipment failure. Changing lamps is an ordinary part of equipment operation. It would be well for anyone, while learning to operate the equipment, to learn at the same time how to change the projection lamps.

Beyond this, a maintenance philosophy should guide the teacher's actions. If a piece of audiovisual equipment does not work during pre-class check-out, there should be a procedure for trying to find common causes of difficulty and simple remedies. First echelon maintenance consists of checking to see that the power cord is plugged into the wall and that the proper switches are turned on. Operating instructions should be printed in a performance prompting style and affixed to the cover of the particular piece of equipment. If all of the instructions are followed and all proper checks are made and the equipment still does not work, a tap of the hand on the side of the case just might do the trick. But this is the end of first echelon maintenance; the major problems should be left to the experts. The temptation to use a screwdriver to find out what restorative miracles can be wrought on the spot should be resisted. The equipment maintenance staff in the school building or in the school system center, outside contractors, or audiovisual dealers would rather have a concise description of the difficulty than a cardboard box full of parts, resulting from inept in-class attempts at repair.

Finally, the teacher should learn to discriminate between equipment that is operating properly and that which is not. An overhead or slide projector without a working fan will drastically overheat. A dirty shutter-gate on a motion picture projector may scratch an entire film, and a projector with a bent film guide may wreak havoc with sprocket holes. Above all, the teacher should not put a broken projector back into supply without indicating this situation to the audiovisual office. To do so merely pushes trouble onto someone else, for projectors will not repair themselves on the shelf.

Finally, a maintenance philosophy includes proper preventive care at regularly scheduled intervals, and the immediate availability of associated items such as spare projection lamps, plug adapters, proper extension cords for power and remote control operation, and extra lenses for varying projection conditions.

Today the classroom teacher, with the support of a well-organized instructional media center and well-trained professional media specialists and paraprofessionals, is in an unparalleled position to provide interesting, flexible, varied, and effective learning experiences for pupils in all grades and in all kinds of school systems.

Educational
Media Bookshelf

Bridges for Ideas, Professional Handbook Series
    Basic Design and Utilization of Instructional Television
    Instructional Display Boards
    The Overhead System
    Local Production Techniques
    Production of 2 x 2 Slides
    Lettering Techniques
    Educational Displays and Exhibits
    The Tape Recorder
    Better Bulletin Boards
    Models for Teaching
    Using Tear Sheets
    Paperback editions, $2.50 each
    Instructional Media Center
    University of Texas at Austin
    Drawer W, University Station
    Austin, Texas 78712

Brown,
Lewis,
and
Harcleroad

AV Instruction: Media and Methods
    by James W. Brown, Richard B. Lewis, and Fred F.
        Harcleroad
    3d ed. 1969   621 pp. $11.50
    McGraw-Hill Book Company
    330 West 42nd Street
    New York, New York 10036

Brown
and
Norberg

Administering Educational Media
    by James W. Brown and Kenneth D. Norberg
    1965   357 pp. $8.50
    McGraw-Hill Book Company
    330 West 42nd Street
    New York, New York 10036

Brown

Selected Readings in Educational Media
    Edited by Walter L. Brown
    1968   110 pp. $3.75
    Simon and Schuster
    Selected Academic Readings Division
    1 West 39th Street
    New York, New York 10018

Costello   *Teach with Television: A Guide to Instructional TV*
and   by Lawrence F. Costello and George N. Gordon
Gordon   2d ed. 1965   192 pp. $5.95
              Hastings House, Publishers
              10 East 40th Street
              New York, New York 10016

              Creative Teaching with Tape
              1970   40 pp.   Free
              Mincom Division/3M Company
              3M Center
              St. Paul, Minnesota 55119

Dale   *Audiovisual Methods in Teaching*
              by Edgar Dale
              3d ed. 1969   736 pp. $11.95
              Holt, Rinehart & Winston
              383 Madison Avenue
              New York, New York 10017

Diamond   *A Guide to Instructional Television*
              Edited by Robert M. Diamond
              1964   304 pp. $8.95
              McGraw-Hill Book Company
              330 West 42nd Street
              New York, New York 10036

Eboch   *Operating Audiovisual Equipment*
              by Sidney C. Eboch
              1968   76 pp. $2.95
              Chandler Publishing Company
              Distr. by International Textbook Company
              Scranton, Pennsylvania 18515

              Elements in Visual Literacy
              Kodak Publication No. AT-25 Free
              Eastman Kodak Company
              Rochester, New York 14650

Erickson   *Administering Instructional Media Programs*
              by Carlton W. H. Erickson
              1968   660 pp. $17.50
              The Macmillan Company
              866 Third Avenue
              New York, New York 10022

Erickson   *Fundamentals of Teaching with Audiovisual Technology*
              by Carlton W. H. Erickson
              1965   400 pp. $8.50
              The Macmillan Company
              866 Third Avenue
              New York, New York 10022

Feyen
and
Wigal

Screen Experience; an Approach to Film
Edited by Sharon Feyen and Donald Wigal
for the National Curriculum of the
Journalism Education Association
1969 286 pp. $5.95
George A. Pflaum, Publisher
38 West Fifth Street
Dayton, Ohio 45402

Gerlach
and
Ely

Teaching and Media: A Systems Approach
by Vernon S. Gerlach and Donald P. Ely
(In press 1970)
Prentice-Hall, Inc.
Englewood Cliffs, New Jersey 07632

Glaser

Teaching Machines and Programmed Learning II
Edited by Robert Glaser
1965 831 pp. $11.50
Department of Audiovisual Instruction, NEA
1210 Sixteenth Street, N. W.
Washington, D. C. 20036

Griffith
and
MacLennan

Improvement of Teaching by Television
Edited by Barton L. Griffith and Donald W. MacLennan
1964 238 pp. $4.00
University of Missouri Press
Columbia, Missouri 65201

Herman

*Educational Films: Writing, Directing, and Producing
for Classroom, Television, and Industry*
by Lewis Herman
1965 338 pp. $5.95
Crown Publishers, Inc.
419 Park Avenue South
New York, New York 10016

Highlights of Schools Using Educational Media
2d pr. 1969 306 pp. $3.00
National Education Association Stock No. 071-02894
1201 Sixteenth Street, N. W.
Washington, D. C. 20036

Kemp

Planning and Producing Audiovisual Materials
by Jerrold E. Kemp
2d ed. 1968 251 pp. $8.50
Chandler Publishing Company
Distr. by International Textbook Company
Scranton, Pennsylvania 18515

Knirk
and
Childs

Instructional Technology: A Book of Readings
Edited by Frederick G. Knirk and John W. Childs
1969 300 pp. $5.95
Holt, Rinehart & Winston
383 Madison Avenue
New York, New York 10017

Lange

Programed Instruction
The Sixty-sixth Yearbook of the National Society
for the Study of Education
Edited by Phil C. Lange
1967   334 relevant pages $5.00
University of Chicago Press
Chicago, Illinois 60637

Mager

Preparing Instructional Objectives
by Robert F. Mager
1962   75 pp. $1.75
Fearon Publishers
2165 Park Blvd.
Palo Alto, California 94306

Markle

Good Frames and Bad: A Grammar of Frame Writing
by Susan Meyer Markle
2d ed. 1969   308 pp. $5.95 paper $8.95 cloth
John Wiley & Sons, Inc.
605 Third Avenue
New York, New York 10016

Movies with a Purpose
28 pp.   (paperback)   Free
Motion Picture and Education Markets Division
Eastman Kodak Company
Rochester, New York 14650

**Pearson
and
Butler**

Instructional Materials Centers: Selected Readings
Compiled by Neville Pearson and Lucius Butler
1969   345 pp. $6.00
Burgess Publishing Company
426 South Sixth Street
Minneapolis, Minnesota 55415

Pipe

Practical Programming
by Peter Pipe
1966   70 pp. $1.95
Holt, Rinehart & Winston, Inc.
383 Madison Avenue
New York, New York 10017

Pula

*Application and Operation of Audiovisual Equipment
in Education*
by Fred John Pula
1968   360 pp. $7.95
John Wiley and Sons, Inc.
605 Third Avenue
New York, New York 10016

Reid   *Research in Instructional Television and Film: Summaries*
and   *of Studies*
MacLennan   Edited by J. Christopher Reid and Donald MacLennan
                     Foreword by Leslie P. Greenhill
                     1967   216 pp. $1.25
                     Superintendent of Documents Catalogue Number
                        FS 5.234:34041
                     U. S. Government Printing Office
                     Washington, D. C. 20402

Rossi   *The New Media and Education*
and   Edited by Peter H. Rossi and Bruce J. Biddle
Biddle   1966   417 pp. $1.95
                     Doubleday & Company, Inc.
                     501 Franklin Avenue
                     Garden City, New York 11530
                     (Originally published by Aldine Publishing Co.,
                        Chicago, 1966.)

Saettler   *A History of Instructional Technology*
                     by Paul Saettler
                     1968   399 pp. $8.95
                     McGraw-Hill Book Company
                     330 West 42nd Street
                     New York, New York 10036

Schultz   *The Teacher and the Overhead Projector*
                     by Morton J. Schultz
                     1965   240 pp. $8.95
                     Prentice-Hall, Inc.
                     Englewood Cliffs, New Jersey 07632

Scuorzo   *The Practical Audiovisual Handbook for Teachers*
                     by Herbert E. Scuorzo
                     1968   241 pp. $7.95
                     Parker Publishing Company
                     West Nyack, New York, 10994

                Standards for School Media Programs
                     American School Library Association and the
                        Department of Audiovisual Instruction
                     1968 $2.00   Stock No. 381-11850
                     National Education Association
                     1201 Sixteenth Street, N. W.
                     Washington, D. C. 20036

                A Teacher's Guide to Overhead Projection
                     1969   96 pp.   No charge
                     Technifax Education Division
                     Holyoke, Massachusetts 01040

Thorton   *New Media and College Teaching*
and   Edited by James W. Thorton, Jr., and James W. Brown
Brown   1968   186 pp. $8.50 cloth $7.00 paper
            National Education Association
            1201 Sixteenth Street, N. W.
            Washington, D. C. 20036

Weisgerber *Instructional Process and Media Innovation*
            Edited by Robert A. Weisgerber
            1968   569 pp. $7.75
            Rand McNally and Company
            P.O. Box 7600
            Chicago, Illinois 60680

Wittich   *Audiovisual Materials: Their Nature and Use*
and   by Walter A. Wittich and Charles F. Schuller
Schuller   4th ed. 1967   554 pp. $11.95
            Harper & Row, Publishers
            49 East 33rd Street
            New York, New York 10016

Wyman   *Mediaware: Selection, Operation and Maintenance*
            by Raymond Wyman
            1969   208 pp. $3.75
            William C. Brown Company Publishers
            135 South Locust Street
            Dubuque, Iowa 52001

References and Guides for Media Materials and Equipment

Audiovisual Market Place
  Directory of equipment manufacturers, software producers and distributors, professional and trade associations, film festivals and conferences, and reference books.
  Edited by Olga S. Weber
  2d ed. 1970   177 pp. $12.25
  R. R. Bowker Company
  180 Avenue of the Americas
  New York, New York 10036

Audiovisual Equipment Directory
  Issued yearly $7.00 to non-profit groups
  National Audiovisual Association, Inc.
  3150 Spring Street
  Fairfax, Virginia 22030

EDUCATORS GUIDE SERIES: Educators Progress Service, Inc.
  Box 97
  Randolph, Wisconsin 53956

  Elementary Teachers Guide to Free Curriculum Materials
  Edited by Patricia H. Suttles
  1968   312 pp. $9.75

  Educators Guide to Free Filmstrips
  Compiled and edited by Mary Foley Horkheimer and John W. Diffor
  1968   139 pp. $8.50

  Educators Guide to Free Tapes, Scripts, and Transcriptions
  Compiled and edited by Walter A. Wittich
  1968   167 pp. $6.75

  Educators Guide to Free Films
  Compiled and edited by Mary Foley Horkheimer and John W. Diffor
  1968   784 pp. $10.75

8mm Film Directory
    Compiled and edited by Grace Ann Kone
    Educational Film Library Association
    1968   532 pp. $10.50
    Comprehensive Service Corporation
    250 West 64th Street
    New York, New York 10023

Guides to Newer Educational Media: Films, Filmstrips, Kinescopes, Phono-discs, Tapes, Programmed Instruction Materials, Slides, Transparencies, Video-tapes
    by Margaret I. Rufsvold and Carolyn Guss
    2d ed. 1967   62 pp. $1.50
    American Library Association
    50 East Huron Street
    Chicago, Illinois 60611

NICEM Media Indexes (data from National Information Center for Educational Media at the University of Southern California)
    R. R. Bowker Company
    1180 Avenue of the Americas
    New York, New York 10036

    Index to 16mm Educational Films
    2d ed. 1969 $39.50

    Index to Overhead Transparencies
    1969 $22.50

    Index to 8mm Motion Cartridges
    1969 $19.50

    Index to 35mm Educational Filmstrips
    2d ed. 1969 $34.00

SERINA FILM LOAN GUIDES: Serina Press
    70 Kennedy Street
    Alexandria, Virginia 22305

    Guide to Government-Loan (16mm)
    First Edition 1969-1970   130 pp. $4.95

    Guide to Foreign Government-Loan Film (16mm)
    First Edition 1969-1970   133 pp. $4.95

    Guide to Military-Loan Film (16mm)
    First Edition 1969-1970   149 pp. $4.95

    Guide to State-Loan Film (16mm)
    First Edition 1969-1970   56 pp. $1.95

Periodicals in Educational Media

*AUDIOVISUAL INSTRUCTION, ten issues years, $8.00 per year
  Department of Audiovisual Instruction
  1201 Sixteenth Street, N. W.
  Washington, D. C. 20036

*AV COMMUNICATION REVIEW, quarterly, $8.00 per year
  Department of Audiovisual Instruction
  1201 Sixteenth Street, N. W.
  Washington, D. C. 20036

EDUCATION AGE, five issues yearly, $2.00 per year
  3M Education Press
  Visual Products Division
  3M Company, 3M Center
  St. Paul, Minnesota 55101

*EDUCATIONAL BROADCASTING REVIEW, quarterly, $6.00 per year
  National Association of Educational Broadcasters
  1345 Connecticut Avenue, N. W.
  Washington, D. C. 20036

EDUCATIONAL/Instructional BROADCASTING, monthly, $15.00 per year
  647 North Sepulveda Boulevard
  Los Angeles, California 90049

EDUCATIONAL SCREEN AND AV GUIDE, monthly, $5.00 per year
  434 South Wabash Avenue
  Chicago, Illinois 60605

EDUCATIONAL TECHNOLOGY, monthly, $18.00 per year
  456 Sylvan Avenue
  Englewood Cliffs, New Jersey 07632

EDUCATIONAL TELEVISION, monthly, $8.00 per year
  140 Main Street
  Ridgefield, Connecticut 06877

ETV NEWSLETTER, bi-weekly, $40.00 per year
140 Main Street
Ridgefield, Connecticut 06877

MEDIA & METHODS, nine issues yearly, $5.00 per year
134 North 13th Street
Philadelphia, Pennsylvania 19107

MODERN MEDIA TEACHER, five issues yearly, $5.00 per year
38 West Fifth Street
Dayton, Ohio 45402

*NSPI JOURNAL, monthly, $20.00 per year
National Society for Programmed Instruction
715 Stadium Drive
San Antonio, Texas 78212

*Official publication of indicated association, with special subscription rates in con-
nection with membership plans.

Media Materials on Media

Educational Media Kit
  Developed by Jerrold E. Kemp and Richard B. Lewis
  Complete kit, $800.00   18 sub-kits available separately
  McGraw-Hill Book Company
  330 West 42nd Street
  New York, New York 10036

Media Programs for Individual Schools
  Filmstrip and recorded narration
  $10.00 complete package
  Publication Sales Section
  National Education Association
  1201 Sixteenth Street, N. W.
  Washington, D. C. 20036

NAEB Instructional Television Demonstration Kits
  Developed by Dr. C. R. Tettemer
  30-minute 16mm sound black and while motion pictures with teaching
    guides

  1. What Television Brings to the Classroom
  2. Role of the Classroom Teacher
  3. Preparing the Television Lesson
  4. Promising Practices
  5. A Case Study in an Elementary School
  6. Examples in Secondary Schools

Rental: $10.00 per kit for one-week period
15-year-lease: $150.00 per kit
Communication Division
101 Lowden Hall
Northern Illinois University
DeKalb, Illinois 60115

Programming Is a Process: An Introduction to Instructional Technology
    by Susan M. Markle and Philip W. Tiemann
    32-minute 16mm sound color film with Instructor's Guide and Viewer
        Handouts
    Rental: $12.00 plus postage for 3 days
    Purchase: $160.00
    Viewer Handouts: $1.00 per set of 20
    Instructional Materials Availability Center
    Office of Instructional Resources
    University of Illinois at Chicago Circle
    Box 4348 Chicago, Illinois 60680

Index